Welcome to the I

This book is designed to help you, your family, friends, co-workers, and customers achieve new levels of joy and impact at work. Every chapter starts with a QR code you can scan with your cell phone to watch my video introduction of the chapter. If you cannot scan QR codes with your phone you can watch the chapter video introductions on my YouTube Channel: DEREK YOUNG.

I look forward to hearing how this book helps you and the people in your network make a legendary impact and find lasting joy!

To stay in touch with me and stay abreast of current and future books and programs, join my network at:

www.store.derekyoungspeaks.com

Be Legendary!

DY

Praise for Derek Young's *Make My Hindsight Your 20/20*

"DY has a unique, entertaining and highly effective method of pinpointing the messages that most leaders looking to seriously reinvigorate their organization's culture need to hear. His wisdom is both practical and insightful. Prepare yourselves for a 'seatbelt session' that I know you will enjoy".

—Kenneth L. Washington
President, Practice Operations
HCA HEALTHCARE
Physician Services Group

"*Make My Hindsight Your 20/20* is an outpouring of Derek's insights around how properly integrated systems position you better for success than simply setting goals. From his oeuvre, I appreciate that goals are for short term projects, while these systems of hindsight allow one to build on success over time. This book is a master stroke."

—Dr. Matthew Walker, III
Professor of Biomedical Engineering and Radiology
and Radiological Sciences
Associate Director of the Medical Innovators Development Program
Vanderbilt University School of Engineering and Medicine

"Derek's wisdom comes from his vast experience and his gift of perception based on observation of human interaction. He has served me and my agency with his skill and insight to help us live our calling. This book is a road map to understanding one's self and creating your best you."

—David Rausch
Director
Tennessee Bureau of Investigation

"Derek Young's book is both practical and insightful. He uses creative nuggets of leadership wisdom, challenging us to be our authentic best. Derek has an impressive track record in inspiring young people and seasoned leaders to achieve their best (including hundreds of Girl Scout executives). This book captures his wit and wisdom."

—Kathy Cloninger
CEO Emeritus
Girl Scouts USA

"DY's 'Hindsights' from his legendary journey is a must-read for leaders at all levels."

—Juan Williams
Commissioner
State of Tennessee Department of Human Resources

"As leaders, we're all looking for ways to increase the level of engagement with our co-workers. In *Make My Hindsight Your 20/20*, Derek Young captures many of the stories and much of the wisdom he's gained over the last 40+ years. He shares many pragmatic, accessible tips that will help our leaders broaden their thinking about what our co-workers really want and desire from us. Derek has always been one of the highest-rated speakers at our leadership meetings. It's great to see he's captured, in book form, many ideas that will help us all be better leaders!"

—Michael J. Packnett
President & CEO
Parkview Health

"This book serves as both a roadmap for becoming an authentic leader and bringing out the best in others. Derek Young provides sound and practical guidance on how to make the most of every day and significantly impact the lives of others in a meaningful way. Every page provides valuable information based on Derek's years of experience. Don't be surprised if you find yourself laughing out loud or wiping away a tear. This is a must read for emerging and seasoned leaders of all ages!"

—Ryan Miller
Executive Director
Habitat for Humanity of Ohio

Make My Hindsight Your 20/20

52 INSIGHTS FOR MILLENNIALS SEEKING JOY AND IMPACT IN A
WORK WORLD BUILT BY BOOMERS

DEREK "DY" YOUNG

www.TrueVinePublishing.org

Make My Hindsight Your 20/20
52 Insights for Millennials Seeking Joy and Impact in a Work World Built by
Boomers
By: Derek Young

Published by True Vine Publishing Company
P.O. Box 22448
Nashville, TN 37202
www.TrueVinePublishing.org

ISBN: 978-1-7336315-5-6

Cover Design by Symmetry Media Group

For more information about the author or to book Derek Young for speaking engagements, visit: www.DerekYoungSpeaks.com

Dedication

This book is dedicated to the four most important women in my life.

My grandmother, the late Grace Young, was my source for love, joy, and security. Her wonderful blend of wisdom, strength, dutifulness, and playfulness enriches my life every day. My granny is the person who shaped my discernment and my love for family.

Other than my wife, my three favorite people of all time are Paul the Apostle, Martin Luther King Jr., and my mother, Jennie Young. She is the perfect mother in my eyes. Never have I seen a person so loving, so consistent, so talented, and so loyal. I am what I am because of who she is.

Third is my mother-in-law, the late Mary Parker. She was as devoted as any Christian, wife, mother, and educator could be. She set the standard for personal, professional order and decency. I am forever thankful to her (and my father-in-law, who was more like a father, the late Kelly Parker) for raising such a wonderful daughter.

The fourth significant woman is my wife, my love, my best friend, and my business partner, Allyson Young. She is the model of the "Proverbs 31 Woman". I thank God for allowing me to build a life with a person so beautiful, so caring, so intelligent, and so elegant. Life is indescribably better for me, our four children—Kayla, Kelton, Kendall, and Kristianna—and everyone she impacts because of her godly character and influence.

Introduction

'Hindsight is 20/20'
Meaning: Looking back at a situation or event that occurred and having a clearer understanding of it and how it could have been done better.

Whether you work in systems engineering in Silicon Valley, real estate in Shanghai, wealth management in London, private nursing in Mexico City, or petrochemicals in Mumbai, you have probably asked some version of this question: *"How do I enjoy my work and ensure that my efforts are making a difference in this crazy, chaotic, unpredictable, multi-cultural, multi-generational world?"*

The daily barrage of good news, bad news, and fake news, coupled with the overabundance of stories about the world's top overachievers and overcomers challenges people of every age, background and career field to examine how their work is impacting the world. As people consider the thousands of hours they will devote to working over their lifetime, they decide they want to be able to look back on a career of significance.

Enter *Make My Hindsight Your 20/20!*

This book is designed to help you answer the aforementioned question. Since joining the professional world 35 years ago, I have steadily sought the answer to this question with varying levels of success. As a 30-year

9

management consultant, leadership trainer, keynote speaker, executive coach, and team leader for some of the world's greatest organizations, I have helped and observed thousands of leaders and employees answer this question. During that time, I have been collecting and sharing many of my most valuable discoveries.

A famous adage says, "smart people learn from their mistakes and wise people learn from the mistakes of others". This book is designed to help you learn from the mistakes and the successes of others. *Make My Hindsight Your 20/20* is a compilation of 52 insights— proven mindsets and methods gained from a plethora of successes and hindsights. My clients, coworkers, peers, and I have used these insights to maintain love for our work and leave a positive legacy in the process.

The insights have helped a wide array of leaders and employees achieve their personal and professional goals in an even wider array of work settings. The insights are grouped into nine chapters to help you "know now, what we wish we had known then". The insights can be read in any order at any point during the year.

Throughout the book you will see references to my Culture Strategy Programs. Since 1987, I have been designing and delivering speaking, training, coaching, and performance management strategies that help individuals and organizations achieve legendary performance. Culture Strategy Programs combine services from each of those areas to help organizations rapidly transform their culture to improve their performance. The trainings are divided into categories such as: culture and leadership development, diversity and inclusion, executive presence, and strategic execution.

I have a catalog of more than 80 Culture Strategy Programs. All of the programs contain hindsights like the ones offered in this book. I hope to share one or more of those programs with your organization someday.

The book has two more important features to help you extract what you need to increase your joy and impact at work. Each chapter begins with a video introduction that highlights some of my favorite aspects of the related hindsights. Each chapter ends with a <u>Traffic Light Action Plan</u> so you can immediately record how and when you will apply the nuggets you learned. You will maximize your reading experience by recording what you will start doing, keep doing, and stop doing to increase your success.

As this book positively impacts you, I hope you will become an ambassador for the Hindsight Movement. The Hindsight Movement is about helping millions of people around the world develop the knowledge, skills, and confidence necessary to better control their work life.

As you share this book and its impact on you with others you will become an ambassador for the Hindsight Movement.

Be Legendary!
DY

Table of Contents

CHAPTER 1: DEVELOP A CLEAR PURPOSE

Hindsight #1: It's All About Your Call

Hindsight #2: Establish A Firm Foundation

Hindsight #3: Create a Clear Vision

Hindsight #4: Work for the Guests at Your Funeral

Hindsight #5: Five Greatest Accomplishments

Scan the QR Code for My Personal Introduction to the Chapter!

Hindsight #1: It's All About Your Call

In far too many cases, I have seen career-focused people do everything in their power to be awesome employees who produce amazing results, yet they still feel unfulfilled. In far too many cases, I have seen career-focused people dedicate the most energetic and creative portion of their lives to build and support someone else's dream only to find that their own dreams and aspirations go unrealized. Rather than follow that path, I encourage you to ensure that your career is leading you to your calling.

Calling is a word that seems to be used most frequently for persons who pursue a life of full-time ministry. We use phrases like, he was "called to the ministry." When I consider all the talents and gifts people use to create organizational success, it is clear to me that every person has a calling. Every person has some process, some endeavor, or some impact that they were designed and destined to deliver to the world for the world's greater good. Bruce Wilkinson, author of the *Prayer of Jabez*, uses the concept of your personal territory to address the issue of calling. He defines assigned territory in this way: "My abilities + experience + training + my personality and appearance + my past + the expectations of others."

When thinking about your calling you should ask the question, "What will I do with my dash?" The dash in question refers to the literal dash that appears on a tombstone between a person's date of birth and their date of death. The dash represents all the person did, all that happened to the person and how the person responded to what happened to them. The dash symbolizes the unique way the person chose to live their life. The dash represents how each action adds up to determine how we impacted others. How we use our dash is another way of determining if we fulfilled our calling.

While some people view their career as their calling, I view career differently. I see a career as a series of jobs, businesses and/or volunteer activities that position you to fulfill your calling. For instance, a young woman might graduate from the University of Pennsylvania with a BS degree in accounting and then start working as a financial analyst at a major accounting firm. During her time at the accounting firm, she might develop a passion for serving the local Alzheimer's center because of their great care for her grandmother, who was stricken with that horrid disease.

She might transition to a financial services firm where she manages the analyst team that supports the wealth management division. During her time there, she might become a committed board member of the local Alzheimer's organization while obtaining her Law Degree at night. Later in her career, she might become a Vice President for the wealth management division of a regional bank. Leveraging her personal experience and board experience, she might become an advocate for families dealing with the negative effects of Alzheimer's.

Along the way, she might earn a license to buy and sell securities and attend training that prepares her to identify and secure high-income investment clients. A few years later, in her efforts to combine her professional expertise and her social service passion, she might focus on providing estate planning for families affected by Alzheimer's to ensure they effectively secure and transfer wealth created by the stricken family member. In this scenario, viewing her career as a part of her calling would clearly help this woman combine elements of her work experience and community service to deliver a much broader impact on the lives of others.

When you consider the concept of calling, would you agree that people who live a calling-focused life seem to experience life on a higher plane? Do they seem to extract more out of every single day? Do they seem to have a good blend of being content and being goal-oriented? If you answered yes to these questions, you are in the right place, and this is my wish for you!

Hindsight #2: Establish a Firm Foundation

I have thought if only I could become rich and famous I would live luxuriously in New York knowing famous people eating in expensive restaurants calling long distance anytime I want
—"Luxury" from *Love Poems*, by Nikki Giovanni

Why are there so many stories of wealthy persons who commit unthinkable acts of deception and self-sabotage? Why do we read statistics that say persons engaged in highly honorable professions sometimes choose terrifying ends to offset the pressures associated with their trade? Why do so many of our favorite entertainers who thrill us on stage with their performances, get us through tough times with their lyrics, and delight us with their talents, tend to leave us in such sorrowful ways?

At some level, I wonder if they were able to clarify their calling. How many documentaries do we have to watch before we believe that money (though it really does solve many problems) does not make you happy; or as the four famous lads from London, the Beatles, told us— really "Can't buy me love"?

In studying individuals who achieve amazing levels of financial success while maintaining normalcy and sanity, it seems that they have a "why" that's bigger than the money. They have a "why" that is larger and more important than the fame and the attention they receive. Leaders who make the time to dig deep and identify a calling that guides their choices seem to manage the impact of materialism so much better than those who don't.

In my coaching with leaders at every level, we use these and other questions to help our clients crystallize their calling. I hope you will 'make' some time to answer these questions.

- What are the top five reasons you go to work every day?
- What are the top five reasons you chose the field you're in or does it feel as if the field chose you?
- What aspects of your work give you the most satisfaction and joy?
- What aspects of your work would you eliminate if you could?
- How do you feel about yourself when you accomplish the goals associated with your work?
- Make a list of three famous people who seemed to fulfill their calling.
- How would you define or describe their calling?
- What led them to pursue their calling?
- How did they use their career to fulfill their calling?
- What questions would you ask them if you could conduct an interview?
- What steps are you willing to take to find and fulfill your calling?

HINDSIGHT #3: CREATE A CLEAR VISION

During my time as Director of Leadership Development with Dollar General Corporation, the nation's largest discount retailer, our Chairman, President and CEO, Cal Turner, Jr., taught me that a mission is a short and compelling description of how you live your life or how you run your organization every day. He also taught me that a vision is a major and challenging goal or destination you want to achieve or reach.

One way to differentiate the two concepts is that a mission is ongoing, but a vision has an end point. A common problem among persons who start the pursuit of their goals with drive, tenacity, and focus, but lose that drive along the way is the lack of a clear, compelling vision. Think about that. What's your vision? Where and who do you want to be in five, ten, or twenty years?

Whatever your answer is, creating a vision enables you to develop a larger reason or set of reasons that answer the why behind your daily choices; especially when parameters affecting your choices are complex, challenging, and confusing.

Many of the consistently effective leaders I have met understand the importance of keeping their vision in clear view. Some leaders create a vision board; a collage or collection of pictures, words, and phrases that describes the future they want. Other leaders create a vision book which includes many of the same visual reminders and motivators. By viewing your calling as the larger impact you have been chosen to make on the world, your vision becomes a combination of the major goals you must achieve to produce that larger impact. Think of it this way. The calling is owning a home that makes guests feel warm, safe, and welcome as they enter. The vision associated with that calling is the combination of landscaping, architecture, artwork, and photos used to create the home.

Have you ever made the time (I repeat: made the time) to establish a vision? Many leaders create a different vision for various areas of their life. For example, one vision might be established for your family. Another vision could be established for the department you oversee at work. Another vision could be established for the soccer team you coach.

Part 1: Here are some of the questions we ask our clients to answer to prepare for creating a powerful vision:

- What are your five most important core values?
- What are your top "lines in the sand" that your core values will not allow you to cross?
- What kind of person do you want to be in 5, 10, or 20 years?
- What kind of family and friends do you want in 5, 10, or 20 years?
- What are some of the wisest choices you have seen others make that you want to duplicate?
- What are some of the biggest mistakes you have seen others make that you want to avoid?

- In 20 years, how would you want others to describe your impact on the world?
- What would you want your entry in the history books to highlight?
- Describe the lifestyle you want to have in 5, 10 or 20 years?
- What areas of society or which societal issues would you like to impact most and why?
- Which of your life experiences are most memorable; what do they have in common; and what do they say about you?

Now that you've answered the questions above, step away from them for a few days before you continue.

Part 2: Using the answers from Part 1, complete the following.

- Write a short story that connects all your answers to the questions above.
- Upon completing the story, develop a statement that describes the essence of what you have written. That sentence is your first draft vision statement. Continue to tweak the statement until it motivates and inspires you.

HINDSIGHT #4: WORK FOR THE GUESTS AT YOUR FUNERAL

The first time I attended a funeral was at age 28. I attended that funeral to support one of my INROADS students who had lost her father in a very tragic and unpredictable manner. At that time, I couldn't imagine the pain and confusion she and her family must be experiencing. Why us? Why our husband and father? Why now?

I determined that the best thing I could offer her was my physical presence as a show of my support. After nearly three decades on the planet, this would be my first encounter with a funeral and everything that was common and customary about a funeral. In preparing to attend the funeral, all I knew to do was to wear black and be prepared to offer comfort to my student and her family in the best manner possible. The experience is etched in my mind.

As I approached the funeral home, I was struck by the number of other people approaching the funeral home, who were neither somber nor wearing black. In fact, several people were laughing and chatting as if they were attending the monthly Rotary Club meeting. I was taken aback. This was a sad occasion. My student had lost her father. Her mother had lost her husband. A group of co-workers had lost a teammate. Why would anyone be smiling, laughing, or joking?

As I entered the sanctuary the air was filled with soft, attention-keeping music and light whispers from groups of two or three people sitting together. The only sound that broke that pattern was the occasional sound of crying and sniffling. Before I could decide what to do next, an usher nudged me to walk down the center aisle of the sanctuary to "view the body" and "pay my respects" to the family. This was a practice I had only seen in movies.

As I looked ahead and saw the father prominently positioned in a beautiful and stately casket, my eyes immediately moved to my student, her mother, and the rest of her family. Suddenly, I was more interested in letting them know that I was there and that I would be there for them in the days and months to come. After brief hugs and condolences with the family, I followed the line of supporters to find a seat. Within a few moments a group of men all wearing matching blazers came before us and formed a circle in a manner that seemed both ceremonial and tributary. They were the fraternity brothers of my student's father. Just as quickly as they formed the circle, they started to sing a song for their departed brother.

Following that, several people took turns sharing a myriad of acknowledgements and words of comfort. Then, just as the minister stood to deliver the first eulogy I had ever heard in person, a lightning bolt of realization struck me: "once you're gone, you're gone." If you want to do something or become something, you better get on with it now!

I know I heard the eulogy, and I know I heard the remaining remarks; but I can't remember them the way I remember that strong revelation. I thought about my student's father and about every other person who had left this world way too soon. What words do they wish they had shared with others? What goals do they wish they had pursued? What relationships do they wish they had fostered?

Likewise, my mind was filled with the thoughts and feelings of the people in the room; the people who were there to celebrate the life of a husband, father, son, brother, nephew, employee, boss, co-worker, church member, fraternity brother, and friend. His funeral was filled with wonderful perspectives and stories from every compartment of his life.

For the first time, I was witnessing how people express their heartfelt regard for another person. The funeral proceedings enabled me to visualize a process that seemed to answer the major question, "what is the purpose of life?" Each person's comments confirmed for me that the purpose of life is to leverage your knowledge, talent, skills, resources, and network to positively impact as many people as possible. In later years, I came to say that the purpose of life is to find and fulfill your calling from God so that you can hear, "Well done good and faithful servant" (Matt. 23:23, KJV) as you enter heaven.

As I left the funeral and returned to my car, I immediately realized that this experience had led me to add a significant layer to my calling and my vision.

A few short years after this experience, I added another significant layer to my calling and my vision. It happened during a radio broadcast by Dr. James Dobson.

During the broadcast, Dr. Dobson said something that simultaneously helped me reflect on my experience at my first funeral and envision what I wanted for my future.

When the co-host asked Dr. Dobson the question, "What are some of the major mistakes business-people make during their children's younger years?" Dr. Dobson said, "I'm sure no one on their deathbed is thinking 'I could have spent more time at the office.'" Whoa! Wait a minute! What did that mean for me as a young man who was not married and did not have children?

How was I living my life? How should I live my life? How would I handle making time for my eventual wife and children? Looking back on that revelation and considering my one-to-one work with thousands of executives and leaders there is a common realization that strikes most of them but sadly not all of them. That realization is that Dr. Dobson's statement is true. Since we don't know when our lives will end, it seems paramount that we become much more serious about our impact on the world and more importantly, our impact on the people we care about most.

As you think about your life and your career, also consider who will attend your funeral (or whatever ceremony or process you select to accompany your transition out of this life). No matter how smart you are, how hard you work, or how much you attain, my guess is that none of your bonus checks will attend your funeral. I seriously doubt that any of your KPIs (Key Performance Indicators) will sign the funeral guest book; and I certainly do not believe your newly acquired luxury car will break in to sign the guest book either.

In their book, *Life Is a Gift: Inspiration from the Soon Departed*, my friends, Dr. Bob Fisher, President of Belmont University, and his wife Judy Fisher, share compelling insights on making your life count from hospice patients who are fast approaching the end of their life. During a meeting where Dr. Fisher referenced the book, he shared a picture of a skeleton wearing a fancy hat, expensive jewelry, and other material items with the caption: "you can't take it with you."

I am grateful. Thanks to the heartfelt messages of the family and friends of a father who left us too soon, a 19-word statement from a national radio broadcast, the written lessons of people at the end of life, and countless conversations with leaders about their personal and professional priorities, I am convinced we should not live for the stuff we can mount up but we should live our lives for the people who will attend our funeral.

We use the following questions to help our clients who are seeking greater clarity on their personal and professional priorities. Answering them will help crystallize your calling:

- What are the most impressive awards and recognitions you have received?
- Who were the persons most central in helping or supporting you to receive those awards and recognitions?

- Who are the three best bosses, coaches, and teachers who positively impacted your life and why?
- What are some of the most important life and work lessons you have learned from your family, friends, and work associates?
- What would you want persons from each of the following categories to say about you if asked to describe your legacy: parents, spouse, children, siblings, grandparents, aunts/uncles, closest friends, other friends, boss, co-workers, direct reports, mentees, and others?

HINDSIGHT #5: STUDY YOUR FIVE GREATEST ACCOMPLISHMENTS

In my efforts to help leaders achieve professional success, it has been extremely helpful to keep shining a light on the internal factors that motivate them to succeed. Though this step may seem simplistic and overly obvious to some, the world offers countless examples of leaders who have worked their heads off for years only to get to the top of the proverbial ladder that was leaned against the wrong building.

One approach that can help leaders clarify their 'why' is the process of identifying their greatest accomplishments. Writing and then studying what *you* deem to be the most significant accomplishments in your life is a great tool for putting first things first because it offers another way to see your values in broad daylight.

Schedule some time to write your list. Consider using the following questions to dig a little deeper:

- What do your accomplishments say about your obvious and hidden talents and gifts?
- What are the common motivators that drove you to reach those accomplishments?
- How does your current work relate to what you see in your top accomplishments?
- What kind of people seem to be common in your top accomplishments?
- What questions do you have about your past, your present, and your future?

DY TRAFFIC LIGHT ACTION PLAN

Your willingness to be hungry, humble, honest, and helpful in your growth process will positively impact you and everyone you encounter. Take time to review your thoughts and notes to identify the insights that struck you.

Use the Traffic Light Action Plan to convert those insights into action steps you will Start Doing, Keep Doing, and Stop Doing. Use your calendar to plan when, how, and where you will take action!

START DOING	WHEN, HOW, WHERE

KEEP DOING	WHEN, HOW, WHERE

STOP DOING	WHEN, HOW, WHERE

Chapter 2: Maintain a Strong Mentality

Hindsight #6: Develop Your Leadership Philosophy

Hindsight #7: Develop Your Four Standards

Hindsight #8: Clarify the Three D's

Hindsight #9: Your Little Voice Knows Best

Scan the QR Code for My Personal Introduction to the Chapter!

Hindsight #6: Develop Your Leadership Philosophy

One of the most valuable, yet often overlooked elements of a leader's promotability is the development and use of a leadership philosophy. How many times have I seen a person receive an interview for a next level opportunity only to be turned away in the end because their answers weren't sharp, or their examples lacked punch, or they couldn't provide the strategic view of 'how' they executed initiatives?

My commitment to helping leaders at all levels of an organization create a leadership philosophy blossomed during my time as a training manager for Dollar General Corporation. During an incredible growth phase where the number of new stores was exploding, the company was searching externally and internally for men and women who could take on the leadership of rapidly growing store districts.

As is common in fast growing organizations, the pace was so rapid that there were not enough internal candidates who were ready to take on next-level roles. Imagine the challenges associated with transitioning from peer manager to district manager, transitioning from running one store to overseeing the performance of ten to fifteen stores, or transitioning from addressing employee issues for seven people to the complexity of issues arising from a group of more than a hundred people.

Like every other rapidly growing organization in the world, we looked to current store managers to fill the new district manager roles (and looked to assistant store managers to then fill the slot that would be left vacant by their newly promoted supervisor). Great idea. Great concept. One problem: Many of the store managers had not taken the time to develop their leadership philosophy. They had not taken the time to conceptualize, summarize, or simply write down how and why they do what they do. Like many leaders, they duplicated what they learned from previous leaders or they managed situations by pure instinct. The problem was always amplified in the interview process.

Often the interviews of store managers for district manager positions produced great frustration for everyone involved. This resulting frustration did not occur because our store managers were not committed to their work. They were. This did not occur because our store managers were not talented people. They were. Finally, this did not occur because our store managers were not equipped to lead larger groups. They were. The issue was that they had not developed the vision, the framework, or the language to explain how they would take on the challenges of a next level assignment.

Since that time, I have shared with many clients, mentees, and friends the idea that every time you pursue a role at the next level (whatever that level might be), the interviewer will want to know more about the 'whys' behind how you achieved your results than the description of your results. The interviewer will want to hear more about the strategies you implemented than the tactical steps you took to achieve success.

Why is having a leadership philosophy such an important issue? Here's why: Your leadership philosophy contains your core beliefs about achieving success, your core standards for performance excellence, your historical references that explain why you believe what you believe, a framework for delivering leadership to your team, and a process for helping your team overcome their weaknesses and fears. I have been wildly impressed by the short-term and long-term impact made by leaders who schedule time to craft a thorough leadership philosophy and start sharing that philosophy with the people on their team.

HINDSIGHT #7: DEVELOP YOUR FOUR STANDARDS

It's Monday at 7:39 a.m., and Kelly is sitting in her office typing away. She's working on her third project of the morning. She's been there since 7:05 a.m., working. As the clock continues to tick, it is now 8:14 a.m., and Kelly is still hard at it when her newest direct report, Felix, walks in the office. On his way to his desk, Felix stops to talk with not one, not two, but three of his teammates. This takes fourteen minutes. Kelly knows this because she's been watching the clock in the common area of the office.

Felix finally arrives at Kelly's door at 8:28 a.m. to ask how her weekend went (which is merely a ploy to share the highlights of his weekend). Three NCAA buzzer beater stories, two hilarious YouTube videos, and one college buddy punch line later, Felix finally heads to his desk to start his day. It is now 8:38 a.m., and Kelly is ticked! However, she doesn't show it. She maintains the poker face she gained from Thursday night card games with her dad. She neither shows nor shares her frustration with Felix's blatant disregard for time and timeliness. You see, one of Kelly's leadership standards is timeliness.

Sadly, this scenario plays itself out countless times in offices around the world every day. A leader has a certain standard like timeliness, collaboration, accuracy, or follow -through that one or more of their team members unknowingly violates on a regular basis. Why does this violation keep happening? Here's one reason: The leader never shares or explains the standard.

The most important component of a leadership philosophy is what I call the four standards. Your four standards are your core mindsets and methods you use to drive and measure team performance. Your four standards are the four things you believe will bring your team the most success in the most expeditious way. Because you are the leader of the team, your standards become the norm that all your team members should strive to understand and achieve.

So, here's the key question: How can they live up to standards they don't know? I am still amazed by the number of leaders who have neither crystallized their four standards nor shared them with their team.

Not only is it important that you clearly define each standard, but it is also important that you ensure every team member fully understands how they should live out each standard. Notice that I did not say that it is important to share your standards with your team. Through many years of trial and error, and a periodic bit of success, I have found that "sharing" and "ensuring" are two entirely different things.

The process of ensuring my team member understands my standards might include my team member using analogies that fit her hobbies and interests to demonstrate understanding. Ensuring that my team member understands my standards might also include my team member sharing examples of his accomplishments or mistakes to provide an example of my standards. Leaders who make the time to gain several forms of confirmation that each team member understands their standards increase clarity and connection.

Among the more than 80 Culture Strategy Programs I deliver, my favorite and longest running program is entitled *Framing Your Leadership Legacy* (formerly, *Developing Your Leadership Philosophy*). Among all the steps involved in the program we ask these questions to help leaders clarify their four standards.

- Can you see the benefit of condensing your leadership approach to four standards?
- How can the use of four standards accelerate and expand your ability to drive change?
- List your four standards: the four mindsets, methods, traits, or skills you want every member of your team to master.
- Write a brief definition or description of each standard.
- Schedule one-to-one time with each direct report or key team member to ensure they understand each standard (some leaders have their team members "sign-off" to indicate that the standards are clear).
- One of the fun and valuable steps in the process involves comparing your rating of each team member's performance of the standards to their ratings.

HINDSIGHT #8: CLARIFY THE THREE D'S

During my childhood, I was often amazed by the power and realism of the many movies I watched. I often wondered how movies could impact me in such a rich and meaningful way. As I got older, I began to believe that the answer to two legendarily juxtaposed questions was yes to both: "Art was imitating life" and "Life was imitating art"! Movie after movie kept giving me a behind-the-scenes look at the motivations and desires of the featured characters. Whether the movie setting was a big corporation, a newly formed government, or a family farm, one of the recurring themes was that there are three major ways that leaders treat people in their efforts to win: 1) They *deceive* people; 2) They *dominate* people; and/or 3) They *dignify* people. As you consider some of your favorite movies, I'm sure you are envisioning stories in each category.

In his book *Becoming a Category of One*, my friend and mentor Joe Calloway shares this perspective on the idea of dignifying people: "With all the negative news about business and corporate America that we've seen over recent years, I come away from this project with a renewed faith that doing the right thing works, treating employees and customers fairly and with respect will lead to success, and that the good guys really do win."

Over the years, movies and the true stories they are based on have proven that when a leader's only real motivation is the accumulation of power and money—by any means necessary—all three of the leadership methods above can yield positive financial returns. Sad but true. This is actually very sad. Movies, newspaper headlines, and TV screen crawls regularly reveal the corrupt systems that produce billions of dollars in revenue and profit. Talk show after talk show uncovers the broad and intricate plans and patterns some leaders use to make over, take over, and run over people to ensure they make money.

Thank God for the 'kicker' on the nightly news which shares a positive story about the goodness of people. Think about how you feel when you hear a story about a leader who achieves amazing success by treating their people well. Consider the relief you experience when you learn that a person has become rich by leaving a path of happy and satisfied employees and customers in their wake. Even though I would greatly prefer a world overrun with "kicker-worthy" news stories about people being respected and dignified, the sad reality is that money can be made with all three D's.

HINDSIGHT #9: YOUR LITTLE VOICE KNOWS BEST

Let me cut to the chase. Never…never…never ignore your "little voice" as you deal with a familiar situation or move towards a new opportunity. For those who are Christians, to you I would say: never ignore the Holy Spirit. While each of us might have different views on our spirituality, I don't think I have ever heard anyone disagree with the concept that we all have a "little voice" inside us; that instinctual trigger that lets us know when something seems odd, and we need to proceed with caution.

Study the results of some of your best and worst experiences in every area of your life (Hindsight!). I would imagine that if you could go back to the beginning of how each engagement started, I bet you will remember how your little voice either gave the go-ahead or placed danger signs along the road to let you know that trouble was imminent. I imagine that if you examine what helped you realize you were in a bad situation you will remember the moment when your little voice said something like: "This ain't right!" "Something's not right about him!" or "Are you sure you want to purchase this?"

Is it starting to come to you now? Are you remembering how your little voice really did try to warn you? First, I want you to relax and join the club. All of us have been there. This reminds me of my experience watching the 1999 box office hit from director, M. Night Shyamalan,

The Sixth Sense. The movie featured young Haley Joel Osment and Bruce Willis. It is a movie you do not understand until the final scenes (Spoiler Alert). When the answers to each mystery in the movie are revealed at the end of the movie, you realize that you saw the signs, but you just didn't use the signs to figure out what was going on.

For all your work decisions—both large and small— allow your little voice to help you figure out what is going on around you. During my career, the moments when I failed to listen to my little voice are my least effective moments. How true is that for you?

To help drive this point home I recommend a brief activity that provides valuable insights. List up to five experiences from your past when your decision to ignore your little voice produced negative results then apply these questions:

1. What went wrong in the end?
2. How did this experience negatively affect you?
3. At what point did your little voice start speaking to you?
4. What did your little voice say?
5. What are the common variables in each experience?

Sidebar: Since we're talking about the little voice, we should highlight this concept for persons who are responsible for conducting job interviews. As the person assigned to selecting new talent for your organization, you have a major role. You are the organization's gatekeeper. Your ability to look beyond the fancy words on the fancy resume paper and look beyond the well-rehearsed responses is paramount to the survival of your organization's culture.

I contend that interviewing people for jobs is like considering who you will allow to be responsible for providing in-home healthcare for your ailing grandmother. Here's the bottom line: During any point in the interview process (on-line resume receipt, lobby paperwork completion, first interview, third interview, office tour, etc.) if your little voice says no on a candidate, LISTEN!

DY TRAFFIC LIGHT ACTION PLAN

 Your willingness to be hungry, humble, honest, and helpful in your growth process will positively impact you and everyone you encounter. Take time to review your thoughts and notes to identify the insights that struck you.

Use the Traffic Light Action Plan to convert those insights into action steps you will Start Doing, Keep Doing, and Stop Doing. Use your calendar to plan when, how, and where you will take action!

START DOING	WHEN, HOW, WHERE

KEEP DOING	WHEN, HOW, WHERE

STOP DOING	WHEN, HOW, WHERE

Chapter 3: Surround Yourself with the Right People

Scan the QR Code for My Personal Introduction to the Chapter!

Hindsight #10: True Friends?

More than fifteen years ago, I was doing one of my favorite things. I was speaking to an auditorium full of middle school students, with the goal to inspire them to maximize their talents. The auditorium was packed. It was filled with some of the common audience members I've encountered over the years:

- The eager front-row-sitter, sitting tall and attentive with pen and pad in hand;
- The reluctant, normally slouching middle-of-the room chatterbox, who is much more interested in his conversation with his friend than my speech to the group; and
- The back-row-window-gazer, who is in the room physically but appears to be at recess mentally.

My goal for the talk to the middle-schoolers was to help them understand the concept of friendship. Since 1978, I have worked with thousands of young people from various backgrounds. One of my major beliefs about youth and their ability to thrive in life is that too many young people follow the advice they receive from their peers far more often than they follow the advice they receive from their parents, teachers, and coaches. Moreover, young people assign the position and title of friend to their "acquaintances" way too soon. Way. Too. Soon.

One of my audience members gave me a nugget during my talk that day and brought this point to light. I opened the speech by telling the group I wanted to talk about friendship. I asked for a volunteer to give a perspective on the topic of friendship. As soon as I asked this question, an 8th grader stood up and offered this, "Mr. Young, when you're talking about friendship, it's like Erika is my friend, but Shatika is my true friend." So, I asked the obvious question, "What is a true friend?" Then she shared this, "A friend is someone you know, and you're cool with, but you don't really trust that much. A true friend is like your girl; someone you really trust for real."

I liked her answer. I understood her answer. It was honest, and it resonated with what had been troubling me for years about the way young people (and sometimes we older people) approach friendship. Here's my take on the concept.

Describing someone as a true friend is like making reservations for dinner at a fine restaurant, arriving at the restaurant, taking your seat, hearing the waiter take your drink order, then asking for a glass of 'wet' water. Exactly! If it's not wet, it can't be water. And if the person is not true, you need not consider them a friend.

How does this treatise on friendship relate to you in your career? Take a moment. Assess the people you spend the most time with at your organization. Do you trust them? Do you really trust them? Really? Have they earned your trust? Have they honored your trust? During the 1980s, *Dallas* was one of America's first and most famous nighttime soap operas. The show's protagonist, J.R. Ewing, played marvelously by actor Larry Hagman, was notorious for memorable and villainous one-liners. Among the many J.R. shared during each episode, one that is most memorable is the notion that you, "Keep your friends close and your enemies closer."

Whatever your stance on that, here's a take on friendship that has helped many of the people I have observed. In many circles, the major belief is that you ultimately learn who your friends are when you're down on your luck. Do you believe that? Has that been your experience? Really slow down and reflect, because here's what I have seen. It seems to me that you don't really find out who your friends are when you're at your worst. Your friends just keep doing what they've been doing.

I believe you find out who your friends are when you're at the top of your game, and you're hitting new levels of success. Nothing challenges friendship like success. The age-old story of the crabs in a bucket really makes the point. If a single crab is left in a bucket, it will probably find a way to escape.

If multiple crabs are left in a bucket, they will all probably die in the bucket because they will not help each other out of the bucket. Instead, as one crab tries to climb out, another crab will pull it back. Then as the next crab tries to crawl out, another crab will pull it back. This process will repeat itself until the crabs' collective fate is sealed. Unfortunately, people often do this to each other when they keep pulling each other back into the common "bucket" (the common place or position in life) they share.

This telephone conversation from *When the Game Was Ours* between Larry Bird and Magic Johnson upon Bird learning that Magic had contracted HIV, demonstrates the kind of friendship I am describing.

Bird: "Magic, I'm so sorry."

Magic: "No, it's going to be alright. I have to take some medication and do some different stuff, but I'm going to fight this thing. So, how are the Celtics looking?"

Bird: "Ah, hell, we'll probably kick your #%*@+."

Bird (To his wife Dinah): "He was trying to cheer *me* up."

Seeing someone close to us really hit their stride can often initiate an interesting personal challenge and deeper look in the mirror. In many instances, life is copasetic if our friends are staying in their lane, sharing the same stories they always share, experiencing the same setbacks they always experience, and allowing us to remain in our comfort zone. Sadly, there are certain persons who won't even show up in your life in a meaningful way until you are in trouble. They want to occupy a front row seat when things aren't going right for you. They revel in your misery, your missed opportunity or your mission gone wrong.

The modern term for persons like this is haters. When I think of people who fall into this category, there is an acronym that describes their modus operandi: "HATERS—Hating All Those Earning Real Success".

Unfortunately, this happens all too often. This is not quite the Saul—David connection which I will discuss later. It's more like the Cain and Abel dilemma. Somehow, the upward mobility of the other person hits a deep chord of self-assessment that causes the Hater to be angry and start thinking: "Why didn't I get that opportunity?" "Why haven't I had those exposures?" "I deserve just as much as she does!" Rather than determine a way to improve themselves, Haters choose to use their time, talent, and energy to take out their frustration on the other person.

Be wise in selecting friends and 'true' friends!

Hindsight #11: Develop Your Blow Steam Team

Stress is your enemy. Yes. Stress is your enemy. Would you agree that stress is the silent partner to many of the major killers that take our family members and friends away from us like cancer and heart disease? If that is how you feel, join me in shouting this next idea from the rooftops. We must do everything in our power to avoid letting negative feelings and experiences rest and root in our hearts and minds because they generate loads of stress.

Instead, we must find a confidante (or two, or three) who will allow us to vent. We must make time to release the anger and frustration that occurs during our career journey. I like to call this group your "Blow Steam Team". When I call any of the members of my "Blow Steam Team", the call normally starts with me saying, "Dude!" That is the signal for a call to get something off my chest. Exercising the ability to get negative ideas and experiences off my chest helps me shed the stress of my life.

Who are the people you have called, can call, or should call to get beyond the stressors of your life? I pray that, in addition to relying on a "Blow Steam Team", you start or continue walking, praying, running, etc. to relieve stress.

One addendum to this idea: Please be thoughtful and careful in making a family member part of your "Blow

Steam Team". In far too many cases, I have seen leaders direct so much stress relief towards their immediate family that the impact is slowly devastating. Think about it. If you overwhelm your immediate family with all or most of the stressors that affect you, you might inadvertently accelerate their stress load.

Furthermore, if you share too much negative with your immediate family you might lead them to build up so much disdain for your organization that they give you advice from a place of anger rather than a place of wisdom. Said another way, if you push them to extremely dislike your organization, you might prevent them from giving you wise counsel.

HINDSIGHT #12: READ THIS TWICE

Have I said never trust the person that knows everyone else's business?

In every workplace there tends to be this archetype: a person who knows what's going on with everyone in the office. No matter the level of the other person, no matter the deportment of the other person, and no matter the station of the other person, the 'know it all' has the scoop on their life. Much like the TV character Huggy Bear from the '70's television show *Starsky and Hutch*, this person is the onsite informant. Faster than Google and more extensive than Wikipedia, this person has *the information you want about the people you work with* (this tag line is available for a fee).

In his book, *The Way We Work: How Faith Makes a Difference on the Job*, my friend Dr. Dan Boone, President of Trevecca Nazarene University, describes what he calls, "Conversational Crossroads" found in today's workplaces: the first is Piranha Pond and the second is Gossip Graveyards. Both destinations are overrun with people who know and discuss everything about everyone else."

As an exercise, I want you to picture the person in your office who fits this description. Conjure the sound of their voice. Imagine yourself in a conversation with that person. Are you there? Never trust that person! Did you get that? Should you talk with the person? Yes. Should you interact with the person? Yes. Should you ever share any information or detail that is too private and personal with that person? No. In the words of my oldest son, Kelton: "What *they* don't know won't hurt *you*."

Just don't do it! End of story!

HINDSIGHT #13: GREAT LEADERSHIP LESSON

I repeat... never trust the person who seems to know everyone else's business...unless you want everyone to know your business. Just trust me on this one!

HINDSIGHT #14: MAKE SURE THEY KEEP IT REAL

I'd like to get right to the point on this one. Make sure you maintain a strong connection with people who will not change the way they feel about you or change the way they treat you as you climb the ladder of success. This is a challenging process, but it is a vital process for assertive, ambitious people who want to "keep their feet on the ground and keep reaching for the stars." (If you're not familiar with this saying, enter it in Google to learn about the legendary radio personality known for closing his broadcasts with it).

Consider all the true and fictitious stories about people who found that their success drove people away. In addition, their success led some of the people closest to them to stop providing honest feedback for fear they would lose their bandwagon privileges and benefits.

Of all the books that address this phenomenon, *Impact* by Dr. Tim Irwin is one of my all-time favorites. Dr. Irwin shares numerous stories, statistics, and strategies that empower leaders to keep it real and stay grounded, so their success does not destroy what matters most. Sports organizations have often shared the partnership NBA superstar LeBron James established with some of his childhood friends. In their relationship, he set out for the NBA with a vision to become a global brand while his friends set out to gain expertise in the supportive areas of marketing, law, and branding. As LeBron has continued to climb the ladder of success, his friends have continued to keep it real with him when discussing his public image and his private choices. At the date of this writing, it seems to be working very well for him and for them.

Hindsight #15: Mentors 'And' Sponsors

Would you rather learn from your own mistakes or from someone else's mistakes? If you selected that you would rather learn from someone else's mistakes, here is a suggestion you should consider. Cultivate relationships with mentors. A mentor is a person who *can* and *will* help you reach your goals. A mentor cares about you and what you do. A mentor gets involved in your life and in your learning process. A mentor shares insight and leads you to other people who can help you succeed. *A mentor advises and connects!*

In addition to mentors, many successful people have greatly benefited from sponsors. Just like a mentor, a sponsor cares about you and your actions. A sponsor also gets involved in what you're doing and how you're doing it. And a sponsor shares helpful perspectives and connections. Here's the difference. Mentors advise and connect, but *sponsors place and protect!* While the mentor helps you prepare to move forward, move ahead, and move up, the sponsor proactively pushes you forward, pushes you ahead, and moves you up. In addition, your sponsor works behind the scenes to ensure that no one disrupts your trajectory. I know what you're thinking: "How do I find mentors and sponsors?"

Here are my thoughts on finding a mentor. First, identify three to five mindsets or skills you want to improve: strategic planning, managing difficult people, investing money, etc. Next, identify several people you know or have met who seem like they might be willing to provide insight and ideas on ways to improve your mindsets and skills. Then, request a meeting with them to discuss your area of improvement. Afterwards, send them some form of thanks for sharing their time and perspective.

If you enjoy the discussion and they seem to enjoy talking with you, and if you receive valuable information, ask them to meet again. If they meet with you again and you enjoy and benefit from the discussion, thank them again. Repeat this process. If repeating this process continues to work for you and continues to work for the other person, you have developed a mentor.

While the process of identifying a mentor is clear and direct, the process of identifying a sponsor is not as clear and direct. Sometimes, the person who mentors you evolves into a sponsor. That is a wonderful process. Sponsors tend to be attracted to persons who demonstrate a hunger for growth, a willingness to go above and beyond the call of duty, and a grateful response to the support they receive. My experience is that finding mentors is much easier than finding sponsors. In many cases, it's almost as if sponsors find you. I suggest you pray for and stay on the lookout for both.

DY TRAFFIC LIGHT ACTION PLAN

Your willingness to be hungry, humble, honest, and helpful in your growth process will positively impact you and everyone you encounter. Take time to review your thoughts and notes to identify the insights that struck you.

Use the Traffic Light Action Plan to convert those insights into action steps you will Start Doing, Keep Doing, and Stop Doing. Use your calendar to plan when, how, and where you will take action!

START DOING	WHEN, HOW, WHERE

KEEP DOING	WHEN, HOW, WHERE

STOP DOING	WHEN, HOW, WHERE

CHAPTER 4: MAKE SELF CARE A PRIORITY

Hindsight #16: You'll Probably Never Need a Break

Hindsight #17: Gear Up and Gear Up Again

Hindsight #18: It's All About the Relationship

Scan the QR Code for My Personal Introduction to the Chapter!

Hindsight #16: You'll Probably Never Need A Break

Have you ever had one experience that drastically changed your life forever? Maybe experience is not the right word. The right word might be epiphany or revelation. Whatever the word, it was a late Friday night when one happened to me. As a part of my role as an IN-ROADS counselor, I was tasked with helping high school and college students navigate a myriad of career, academic, and life issues. This was a part of my role that I took seriously; so seriously, that I found myself supporting, coaching, and encouraging students seven days a week and sometimes ten-to-twelve hours a day.

One Friday night, my telephone coaching went late into the evening for a student who was struggling with multiple issues. Nothing the student had done to solve their issues had worked, and nothing I was saying was making a dent in the issue. I persisted by asking, listening, and reframing for two solid hours. Eventually, I finally hit on a perspective that helped the student gain the clarity and confidence necessary to move ahead. As the student ended the call with "Thanks, Mr. Young!" and I hung up the phone, the revelation began. (On a related note, that student is now a brand manager with a Fortune 50 food and beverage company).

As I looked at the phone, realizing that my voice was gone and that I was beyond exhausted, it became clear that if I kept up this pace I would have a bunch of well-counseled students who would be looking for a new counselor because I had been carted off on a hospital stretcher. In an instant the thought struck me, and it has been a guiding principle ever since: *If you take a break before you need a break, you'll probably never need a break.* Let me say that again. If you take a break <u>before you need</u> a break, you will probably <u>never need a break</u>. Suddenly, I could see how many people run and run and push and push, but rarely make time for rest, relaxation, and reflection. And as a result, they often shorten their careers and sometimes shorten their lives.

Another important realization that struck me is that when some people finally decide to make time for rest, relaxation, and reflection, they usually take a break when they're so exhausted that they never gain the benefit of the break. Can you see this in your life? How many tax professionals only take a break in May after the craziest time of their year? How many retail executives wait to slow down only in February after they balance the books in January?

The concept ripped through my mind with so much clarity. The best way to maintain a strong pace *and* maintain my energy and power along the way was to recognize that humans need rest, relaxation and reflection. Think about it. This concept is so important that even Jesus Christ made time for the three R's.

I know that what you do is important. I know that what you do has an impact. Fortunately, top executives, research scientists and home-based business owners alike have bought into this concept of taking a break before they need a break, and they have reaped the benefits.

Think about the number of times you have heard people say, "The work will be there when you get back." To start this process in your life, you might consider identifying a series of simple and varied activities that bring you peace of mind and a smile. Please know that it is important to focus on activities that bring *you* peace and joy.

For instance, I gain a lot from perusing business, architecture, and travel magazines in the grocery store between appointments. It is a process that is not only calming but it often provides a neat insight or perspective on an interesting topic. I enjoy taking a short trip to a high-end men's clothing store to check out recent fashions and styles. Taking a long, unscripted drive on a clear, crisp morning is another one of my favorites.

What helps you chill? Is it a short weekend getaway? Is it reading a book in a local coffee shop? Is it a boat ride on the quietest section of the lake? Whatever your choices, please choose them and commit to keeping them locked in your calendar throughout the year. Here's why. Your work will change week after week, month after month, and year after year. Conversely, you only get one spirit, one mind, and one body. Listen. You only get one spirit, one mind, and one body, which are the only things stress seeks to destroy. That's why this concept of taking a break before you need a break is so important.

HINDSIGHT #17: GEAR UP AND GEAR UP AGAIN

Over the years, I have heard various leaders and employees talk about the importance of getting geared up for the workday. This is one of the most challenging aspects of being a consistently awesome performer because "life happens" to us all. My Culture Strategy Program, entitled *Elvis Is In The Building,* prepares participants (especially leaders who run districts and regions where they do not see the employees on a regular basis) to do whatever it takes—within reason—to put aside troubling personal issues to ensure they are giving their best in each new work interaction.

During my time as Director of Diversity, Inclusion, and Community Outreach for Cracker Barrel, I often asked store employees to consider that once they entered the store wearing the brown Cracker Barrel apron they— just like *Batman*, *Superman,* or *Wonder Woman*—were donning a costume that meant they would transition from their role as Bruce, Clark, or Diana to use their customer service super powers. These super powers include the ability to answer the same question 400 times a day with courtesy and grace; the ability to get a ten-person breakfast order correct and served promptly; and the ability to establish just the right amount of personal connection and responsiveness with hundreds of customers every day.

The thought of gearing up for work is especially true for leaders who work in a multi-unit format and find themselves traveling to interact with different teams they do not see every day. Accordingly, each visit and interaction will carry so much more weight. Interpersonal slights, oversights, and mistakes take much, much longer to discover, repair, and heal. The "Elvis is in the Building' program also helps leaders ask a series of questions that direct them to employ more respectful and focused communication as a tool to create great performance.

Now here's the other side of this important coin. In all the years that I heard people talk about gearing up for work, I also heard them speaking of 'winding down' on their way home. News flash. Your family wants, needs, and deserves the same level of attention, focus, and care that you give to your coworkers, partners, and customers. Guess what that means? They don't want you to wind down. They too want you to gear up! You can gear up for home the same way you gear up for work.

As you make plans to raise your level of performance at work, consider making plans to raise your level of interaction at home by answering questions like these. How will you prepare to give your daughter positive energy as you take your seat on the sideline during her soccer practice? What will you have in your hands when you enter the house: a laptop or a bouquet of flowers to brighten the kitchen? Should you extend your drive around your neighborhood to clear your mind of all the grief you dealt with at work before you go in the house?

My prayer for you is that you reap the professional and personal benefits of gearing up at work *and* gearing up at home.

HINDSIGHT #18: IT'S ALL ABOUT THE RELATIONSHIP

This conversation and the resulting speaking engagement amplifies the importance of relationships.

Church Representative (CR): "Hello Mr. Young. We heard that you're a great speaker, and we would like you to speak to the young people (ages 13 to 22) at our church."

DY: "Certainly. What's the focus of your program?"

CR: "We would like you to inspire them to start viewing their parents, grandparents, and caring elders more as mentors and advisors."

DY: "OK. How much time do I have to speak with them?"

CR: "Thirty minutes."

DY (To self): *Say whaaaaaaat?!*

DY (To CR): "OK. Please send me the date, time, and location of your program".

Quite a request! As a person who appreciates a good challenge, I wanted to take this one on. On my best days, I make time to pray to God and ask for guidance on what to say to any group I have been asked to address. Fortunately, I did that for this group. The insight came, and the message went like this: I asked the group of young people to tell me the name of the most powerful person in America. Almost in unison, they named the current president, Barack Obama. I then asked them a few key questions about the President.

DY: "Do you think he is intelligent?"

Youth: "Yes."

DY: "Do you think he is accomplished?"

Youth: "Yes."

DY: "Do you think he can make decisions on his own?"

Youth: "Oh yes."

DY: "Even though you think all these things are true, is the President a person who uses advisors?"

Youth: "Yes."

DY: "If an intelligent, accomplished, decision-making leader of the free world has advisors and you're 15 years old in the 10th grade, why don't you have advisors?"

Youth: "Whoa!"

I went on to tell the young people that I would imagine that some or even many of their elders—definitely those who are non-tech savvy—could not differentiate a "face-tweet" (Facebook and Twitter) from an "insta-rest" (Instagram and Pinterest). I would imagine that many of their elders might assume an Apple is something you eat, and you Google when you think something is funny.

Then, the life lesson emerged. "Your granny might not understand social media, but I bet she can pick out a liar from a mile away. I bet she can sense when your new main-squeeze (for my younger readers this term is comparable to "your boo") needs to be left on the shelf. And here's the reason why: *times change, terms change, and techniques change, but human nature never changes.*

That's why success in life is all about our relationships.
Lying is still lying. Envy is still envy. Laziness is not a
new concept."

As a leader or employee your understanding of human
nature will do more for your career than any social media
tool ever will. Let's face it, social media experts even base
their strategies on their knowledge of how consumers
think and act. Through the work of many great writers,
thinkers and speakers, we know so much more about human nature and can therefore more predictably improve
the quality of our relationships.

Several months after my time with the young people,
the leader of the group who asked me to speak informed
me that several of the parents and grandparents had no-
ticed a marked improvement in the way their youngsters
approached them and sought their advice. This story reso-
nates deeply with me because in the world of leadership,
your ability to understand and connect with people is
powerful currency. If you have elected to lead others in
decency and respect, this message should resonate with
you. Know that your ability to understand human nature is
the greatest pathway to lead others.

DY TRAFFIC LIGHT ACTION PLAN

Your willingness to be hungry, humble, honest, and helpful in your growth process will positively impact you and everyone you encounter. Take time to review your thoughts and notes to identify the insights that struck you.

Use the Traffic Light Action Plan to convert those insights into action steps you will Start Doing, Keep Doing, and Stop Doing. Use your calendar to plan when, how, and where you will take action!

START DOING	WHEN, HOW, WHERE

KEEP DOING	WHEN, HOW, WHERE

STOP DOING	WHEN, HOW, WHERE

Chapter 5: Keep Growing

Scan the QR Code for My Personal Introduction to the Chapter!

Hindsight #19: Learn the Most Valuable Skill

Have you ever heard the quip that says, "'B' students work for 'C' students and 'A' students teach?" I haven't done the research to know how common this is, but here's what strikes me as an underlying aspect of this statement. How many times have you met an 'A' student who has great, and sometimes hard to fathom technical skills but limited people skills? How many times have you met an 'A' student who can accomplish miraculous mathematical, scientific, or physiological feats, but they can't discern the jealousy of their roommate? In historic and powerful fashion, Dr. Daniel Goleman took the lid off this concept in his seminal offering, *Emotional Intelligence*.

Dr. Goleman's book deftly describes what my mother taught me as a child, "Derek, if you don't learn anything else, you have to learn how to deal with people." Dr. Goleman helped leaders around the world understand that in many, many instances IQ (a measure of intelligence) is not the best barometer for upward career mobility or sustained organizational leadership effectiveness. Instead, the more reliable predictor of strong career impact is "EQ" or Emotional Quotient. EQ is another term for influence or people skills.

Stop right there.

This assertion does not mean that leaders should not possess and pursue high levels of intellect. Intellect is a powerful tool that produces amazing results all by itself. But when intellect is coupled with great influence and great people skills, the results are ultra-phenomenal. Leaders need many skills to achieve success. Picture a leader who has vision, tenacity, creativity, thick skin, energy, drive, endurance, passion, and strength, but lacks influence. Think about it by considering the pathway of some of the people we have crowned as geniuses of their time.

Imagine Beethoven without the ability to influence others to transcribe and disseminate his music. Imagine Edison's bevy of inventions without the ability to influence others to fund, promote, and mass-produce his discoveries. Imagine Steve Jobs' amazing sense of inventiveness without the ability to inspire others to join him in his journey for technological superiority.

Note: While I'm on the topic of geniuses, here's a perspective I'd like you to think about. It seems to me that there are four kinds of people who can regularly get away with being crass, eccentric, and even mean, without feeling the brunt of correction: Geniuses, Founders, Owners and the children of geniuses, founders, and owners. But the rest of us need to be likable; hence, the need for greater influence and people skills.

Step by step, individuals can learn to improve and increase their people skills. When this happens, a life, a career, or an entire organization can be transformed.

HINDSIGHT #20: YOUR BEST ODDS ARE 6 TO 1

In the space below, draw a person's head with two eyes, two ears, two nostrils and one mouth (further decorate it as you choose). Now, below the nostrils and above the mouth, draw a dotted line from the left side of the face to the right side of the face. Take a few moments to study your picture then consider this. There are six 'intake' valves above the line. There is only one output valve below the line. Hold on to that thought.

Have you ever received feedback on a project that led you to do some self-discovery? I remember receiving feedback that caused me to do a deep dive on my own history. I spent a few hours listing, reviewing, and analyzing projects that had stalled or failed (the list got long really). I wanted to uncover the common factors for poor results.

At the end of the process, the answer was simple but quite overwhelming. I realized that in every instance where I failed to succeed, I had not listened well (ears); I had not been very observant (eyes); and I used very little discernment (nostrils). Key lesson: I also realized that in those same instances, I did too much talking (mouth). It was as if a bolt of lightning had struck me when I realized that my lack of discovery time (listening, observing, and discerning) led me to make too many assumptions or misread key relationships.

In his book *What Got You Here Won't Get You There*, Marshall Goldsmith shares that:

> "80 percent of our success in learning from other people is based upon how well we listen. In other words, success or failure is determined before we do anything. The thing about listening that escapes most people is that they think of it as a passive activity. You don't have to do anything. You sit there like a lump and hear someone out. Not true. Good listeners regard what they do as a highly active process—with every muscle engaged, especially the brain. Basically, there are three things that all good listeners do: They think before they speak. They listen with respect. They're always gauging their response by asking themselves, 'Is it worth it?'"

This process was so fruitful and educational, I decided to do the same thing with my successes and victories. What were the common factors in my winning initiatives? What were the consistent steps I took to achieve great results; especially in the face of great challenges and challengers? Guess what. It was just the opposite. In almost every instance when I leveraged what I gained through significant amounts of discovery, I was able to thrive.

Here's the concept in simple terms: *If you will listen, observe, and discern six times as much as you talk, your talking will probably be six times more effective.*

Making this commitment to discovery will help you *say the right things to the right people in the right way at the right time*. If you have recently joined a new team or a new organization, do your best to rely on your intake valves (eyes, ears, and nostrils/discernment) to develop a thorough understanding of your new culture before you inadvertently misuse your output valve (mouth).

Hindsight #21: Going Deeper with Seatbelt Sessions

It was a normal day during a normal work week when one of my Dollar General colleagues burst into my office. He was not my boss. He was not one of my direct reports. He was not a member of my larger team. He had not requested a meeting. He had not even hinted at the need for a meeting. He just showed up in my office, and he did so with great intensity. As he stepped into my office, he kept facing me as he slowly closed the door with his hands behind his back. For a split second, I went into, "I think I can take him" mode. After shutting the door completely, he unloaded his question, "Man, what are you doing?" I was stunned. But before I could speak, he said, "Every time I look up, you're getting another promotion. I want to know what you're doing." Suddenly, I caught up to the purpose of the unplanned, urgent conversation. Since I did not have any pressing priorities at the time and I felt a sense of respect for his direct approach, I offered an answer.

I quickly said, "Seatbelt Sessions!" My visitor looked even more stunned now as he said, "Seatbelt Sessions. What is that?" I told my colleague that once a quarter, every quarter, I scheduled a 30-to-45-to-60-minute meeting with my sponsor (who was also my mentor) and asked one question: "What do I need to fix?" I called these meetings Seatbelt Sessions because I would put on an imaginary seatbelt to keep myself upright and stable during the barrage of realities, perceptions, conjecture, and blind-spot issues my sponsor/mentor would share with me. Though the discussions were often painful and humbling, I conducted them religiously. At the end of each meeting, I would unlatch my imaginary seatbelt, leave his office, and strive to take two important steps:

1. Do everything he suggested starting with the items I disagreed with most; and

2. Thank him *as soon as* I experienced positive returns from his counsel.

Over a seven-year period, this process did not prevent me from making more mistakes. It did not prevent me from facing more challenges. And it did not prevent me from needing additional Seatbelt Sessions. It did, however, supplant my sponsor/mentor's guidance and support as a mainstay in my development, and it propelled me to four promotions and produced higher levels of self-awareness and effectiveness.

Hindsight #22: Dealing with Differences

At the writing of this book, we are witnessing the most culturally diverse workforce of all time. My clients often share their discomfort and unpreparedness to effectively address the numerous diversities that exist in their team. In my Culture Strategy Program, entitled *Winning with Diverse Teams*, I encourage leaders to focus on the behaviors of their teammates rather than try to read their minds. I encourage leaders to identify common areas of interest to establish a connection with employees who appear to be different.

I encourage leaders to become proficient at quickly learning and leveraging the Standard Goals Tree. The concept behind this tool is simple: Even though a leader and employee have different goals, they both have goals; even though a leader and employee might have names that sound different, they both have names; and even though they have different eating customs, they both eat; so forth and so on.

The power of this process is that it helps people relax with each other by realizing they have more in common than they might realize. In my Culture Strategy Program, entitled *The Power of Possible Similarities*, I help clients reframe how they view the few obvious and external differences they see in others to consider the hundreds of things they have to choose from that might be common traits, perspectives, and interests.

By helping people focus on believing and discovering how they share multiple commonalities with people who are 'different', they usually create a pathway to greater work relationships and greater work results.

HINDSIGHT #23: EXPAND YOUR PERSPECTIVE

When I joined INROADS in 1990, it was America's leading non-profit charged with identifying, preparing, and connecting talented African American, Hispanic, and Native American youth with meaningful internships and upward career ladder opportunities in Fortune 1000 companies. This timeframe marked the growth and explosion of the diversity movement. During the past three decades, I have had the great fortune of helping numerous leaders and companies transform their cultural, operational, and financial performance through greater understanding of and commitment to inclusive behavior with their diverse workforce.

Among all the concepts included in the diversity message, one of the most important is the concept of perspective. What is perspective? It's seeing something from a different point of view...whether you agree with it or not.

It's increasing your understanding of another person's or group's opinion and stance...whether you like it or not. Leaders who want to make their pursuit of success in a diverse world and marketplace much easier and much more fluid understand that limiting and narrowing their perspective is a recipe for sameness and smallness. Leaders who realize that broader perspective accelerates their ability to understand, connect with, and influence others—from a wide array of backgrounds—can identify and make decisions that increase the likelihood of their success.

Consider how my perspective on homelessness was altered after learning that the man I periodically saw walking the downtown streets of my city had been the CEO of the company housed in the tallest downtown building.

The tragic and sudden loss of his wife and daughter in a horrific car crash sent him into a personal down-spin. Consider how my perspective on violent youth and adults changed after learning that my angry and combative nine-year-old summer camper never took off his t-shirt (even during swimming) to hide the grotesque scars created after his father put out cigarettes on his back as a form of punishment? How might your perspective change if you broadened it? How might you better understand your most challenging employees if you learned more about their work background?

You might be in a better position to lead your employee who won't make a tough decision after learning how he has been affected by two consecutive insecure, micro-managing supervisors who blocked or overturned every decision he made. You might better understand the buying tendencies of your largest customer segment if you spent a week performing many of the daily tasks they must perform. My most successful clients are those leaders who realize that producing amazing results in a broad world is significantly aided by broader perspective.

DY TRAFFIC LIGHT ACTION PLAN

Your willingness to be hungry, humble, honest, and helpful in your growth process will positively impact you and everyone you encounter. Take time to review your thoughts and notes to identify the insights that struck you.

Use the Traffic Light Action Plan to convert those insights into action steps you will Start Doing, Keep Doing, and Stop Doing. Use your calendar to plan when, how, and where you will take action!

START DOING	WHEN, HOW, WHERE

KEEP DOING	WHEN, HOW, WHERE

STOP DOING	WHEN, HOW, WHERE

Chapter 6: Politics Aren't Bad... People Are

Scan the QR Code for My Personal Introduction to the Chapter!

HINDSIGHT #24: GET READY TO RUN FOR OFFICE

SCENE: A 1st grade recess playground near you.

Evan: "Charlotte, come over here and play catch with me."

Charlotte: "No!"

Evan: "Oh, come on Charlotte. You played catch with me yesterday."

Charlotte: "No, Evan. I don't want to."

Evan: "Fine. I was going to share my chocolate cake with you again."

Charlotte: "No, Evan! I'm already playing with Tessa."

Evan: "O.K. No cake for you. And I won't share my homework with Tessa anymore!"

Tessa: "Throw it to me Evan!"

Charlotte: "No, throw it to me!"

The leader who doesn't want to deal with politics is like the ER doctor who doesn't want to deal with blood. Wherever there are people there are politics. Politics is just a fancy word for the hour-by-hour and minute-by-minute jockeying people do to gain, build, and wield influence with others. The leader who says they don't want to deal with politics should turn in their "leader card" on their way out the door.

Regardless of the industry, the niche, the product or the service, or the playground—like the one referenced above—politics are here to stay. Corporate America has politics. The educational arena has politics. Government?

Really? The nonprofit world has politics. What about the religious world; are there politics there? Just ask a friend who works in that world every day.

Individuals who want to lead others should take a lesson from the front-runners of their local, state, and national political races and get ready to develop their campaign as if they were preparing to run for office. When it comes to dealing with politics, I am reminded of these famous words often uttered by coaches, teachers, and parents when their players, students, and children are overcome by some aspect of life they do not have enough experience or exposure to fully understand: "Get over it!"

HINDSIGHT #25: LET'S CALL 'EM MONEY SKILLS

This book is all about lessons it has taken me 40 years to learn through observation, experience, failure, pain, victory, inquiry and repetition. One of my favorite sayings, which is also one of the most under-applied sayings, is, "This is a people business." I have heard this used in hospitals, car dealerships, administrative offices, retail stores, and funeral homes. I think it's true. Without people, there would be no business. Without people, there would be no Wall Street. Without people, there would be no internet. Without people, there would be no Great Wall, no Alaskan pipeline, no Chunnel.

If these thoughts and statements are true, why do we find that people are still being treated so poorly in organizations of all sizes, structure, and scope? Why do we still find organizations that avoid giving people learning and development opportunities? Why do we have so many workplaces that (even though they don't have to) deny people adequate time to heal from natural, unnatural, and tragic experiences?

Here's one perspective: Someone decided to start calling people skills soft skills. Why? Have you ever tried to untangle the mess caused by a group of entitled, disgruntled employees who have a treasure chest full of institutional knowledge and a land map with the sites of all the buried skeletons? Have you ever been asked to negotiate the competing interests of a powerful union leader and an over-confident corporate executive? Have you ever had to humbly run the PowerPoint presentation for a ranking leader who took 100% credit for an idea you brought to life over 67 consecutive late nights (oh yeah...and you created the PowerPoint too)?

If you can relate to any of these scenarios, you realize that there's nothing soft about what it takes to effectively lead and influence people. And as a result, there is no money without people skills. At the end of the day, every organization thrives based on the way their people perform. Therefore, good people skills should be called good money skills.

Hindsight #26: It's Not What You Know AND It's Not Who You Know

Have you ever experienced this when reading a book? You've been reading several pages with great interest and great comprehension, when suddenly the information on the pages seems to blur. You know that you have read the words, but you probably haven't connected with the author's intent? Well, this is not the time to do that because this is one of the most valuable ideas I can share.

Has there ever been a statement that has been shared more openly and more convincingly by more people than the statement, "It's not what you know; it's who you know"? These are nine simple words that reveal a common lesson that many people wish they had learned earlier in life (Hindsight!). Throughout my life, family members, friends, teachers, bosses, TV characters, and others have used that phrase to amplify the power of strong relationships. I, too, have used the phrase to dissect and then describe various partnerships, promotions, and progressions that have occurred in a wide variety of organizational settings.

Some time ago, I gained a deeper understanding of this colloquialism that I began to use with our clients. As I reflected on my career, I made a startling discovery: Every job I ever had I obtained through a relationship. Wow! Every job? Every job! As a matter of fact, even my transition from high school to college was aided by a relationship. I invite you to back-track your career to uncover the mighty role of relationships (Hindsight!).

Recently, I was reminded of a conversation I had with two friends who were CEOs in the nonprofit community. They were planning a large, annual retreat for a major leadership conference for nonprofit CEOs in the Southeast. They began to discuss their need for a keynote speaker to close the conference with a compelling message on the importance of a winning attitude and a servant -leader mentality. I made the mistake of "thinking" (or should I say "assuming") they knew that I delivered keynote speeches, especially on topics like a winning attitude and servant leadership.

As they continued to discuss the need for a speaker who could end the conference with a strong finish, I began to feel that I was on an episode of *Candid Camera* (a 1960s version of *Punked* for those of the Ashton Kutcher generation or *Impractical Jokers* of current fame). The longer they talked, the more I thought, "They must be joking; they are pulling my leg. They know I would be perfect for that event. They know that would be right up my alley. Surely, they are just teasing me." Ten minutes later, I had to break the uncomfortable silence.

ME: "Uh guys, you know that I'm a speaker right?!"

CEO 1: "What Derek, you do speaking? Wow, I didn't know that. Did you?"

CEO 2: "I didn't know that either."

ME: "You all didn't know I'm a speaker? Both of you have seen me deliver keynotes on several occasions."

CEO 2: "Yes I have, I just didn't know you did that professionally. I thought you did that as a part of your job."

CEO 1: "Same here. How long have you been speaking professionally?"

ME: "Ten years now."

CEO 2: "Well, would you be interested in our event?"

ME: "Certainly!"

The speaking event for the nonprofit leaders was a great success, and a few of the organizations in attendance asked me to speak at future events! See the scenario: I knew them, they knew me, but they did not know what I could do for them.

How many times have you heard someone brag about their contact list full of popular people? At the end of the day, knowing others is great, but achieving great things with and for others seems to be an even greater way to live. Think about it. How many high-level leaders do you know? How many of them have done anything to positively impact you or your career? How many influential people do you know? How many of them have made a phone call on your behalf or signed off on an opportunity for you?

Here's the reality. Knowing someone in authority is good. Knowing persons of influence is cool. The issue is, do they know you, and do they know what you can do? Now, I say it like this: It's not what you know. It's not even who you know. It's who knows what you can do for them and vice versa.

HINDSIGHT #27: MAKE SURE THEY REALLY CAN HANDLE THE TRUTH

Have you ever known a situation when a leader (especially a senior level leader) receives a major epiphany that they want to hear the truth from their team or teammates? Have you ever known in that same situation that the epiphany was *only* an epiphany but not something the person was prepared to carry out?

As I look back, I can see countless situations when someone seemed so genuine and sincere in their search for the truth and their desire for honest and constructive feedback, but once they heard it, they responded poorly (Hindsight!). I sincerely wish I could give you a magic formula to decipher the times when people will truly receive and use the honest feedback they request. I really do. I have seen far too many people experience the pain and embarrassment of the immediate or future retaliatory outburst of anger and frustration from a person who was not satisfied with the 'truth'.

The next time someone tells you they want you to 'keep it real' or to 'bring it' because they can handle it, ask for a quick recess. During that recess, I want you to YouTube the classic scene from the movie *A Few Good Men*, when Colonel Nathan Jessup (Jack Nicholson) tells Lt. Daniel Caffee (Tom Cruise), "You can't handle the truth", in response to Lt. Caffee's ardent request for the truth.

HINDSIGHT #28: KNOW THY UPLINE

Know Thy Upline is the title of one my Culture Strategy Programs. It's a good one because it focuses on one of the most important relationships in a person's life: the employee-boss relationship. More importantly, the program helps participants identify ways to influence that relationship. Among all the things I get to share with my clients, this lesson has probably helped more people earn promotions than any other. Here are some of the things I encourage participants to learn about their boss:

- Top three "behind the scenes" work priorities.
- Top three public business priorities.
- How their upline leaders perceive them.
- Preferred way to receive important information and bad news.
- Preferred information resources.

And the most important item on the list…

- Level of insecurity with team member honesty, creativity, visibility, and advancement.

From my vantage point, there is no factor that has hurt, halted, or hampered organizational progress more than insecure leaders. Think about the leader who needs to take credit for every new idea or discovery. Think about the leader who is unwilling to promote or advance any of the people on their team. Consider the leader who needs to control every aspect of their team's behavior and performance every time they work with other groups. Finally, think about the leader who wants to keep 'pimping' their team members rather than equip them for greater opportunities. *Yes, I said it!*

Among all the famous examples of an insecure leader not being willing to accept and leverage the talent of someone on his team, the Biblical story that describes the relationship between King Saul and his top warrior David is legendary. As the King of Israel, Saul was the man and David was 'the man next to the man'. After Saul led his army to defeat the nation's latest adversary, the reporters said that Saul took out 1,000 enemy soldiers. This was an amazing militaristic achievement.

Those same reporters also said that David took out 10,000 enemy soldiers. Wow! Together, Saul and David took out 11,000 enemy soldiers. As the soldiers walked through their hometown following the battle, Saul could hear the townspeople chanting, "Saul has slain his thousands, and David his tens of thousands" (Samuel 18:7, KJV). Sadly, Saul— operating in total insecurity—did not respond well.

Rather than recognizing David's effectiveness in helping Israel avoid being conquered and enslaved, Saul's insecurity led him to do the unthinkable. He commissioned that David be taken out. Gut check time: how do you think you would have handled that if you were in Saul's shoes? Would you try to annihilate your best soldier (employee) or create a training program where his fighting (work) skills could be duplicated with all the soldiers (employees)? I suggest you periodically take time to evaluate your current boss-employee relationships to determine how you should handle future interactions.

Hindsight #29: Look Before You Leap

Have you ever worked in a setting where the top leader espouses a clear set of decent and admirable core values, but one of the high-ranking or highly visible members of the team seems to violate those values in broad daylight? It's the kind of situation where you ask questions such as, "Why is that person in that position?" "How did that person get that job?" Or, "How does that person still have a job?"

As the diagram below demonstrates, the leader (L) is on the left, representing (or at least publicly declaring) all the wonderful values that are reflected on the organization's website. The person I refer to as the apparent non-conformist (ANC) is on the right, demonstrating behavior unbecoming of the organization's core values.

Diagram 2: YMG Look Before You Leap Chart®

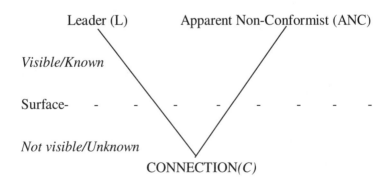

Why do I use the word apparent? I use the word apparent because in some cases, the leader knows exactly what the ANC is doing, why they are doing it, and how they are doing it. Many times, the leader has directed the ANC to act the way they are acting. So, what appears like nonconformist behavior to onlookers, is actually the obedient behavior of a good soldier following the leader's instructions.

The dotted line is the demarcation between the aspects of the Leader-ANC relationship that are visible and invisible. The "C" beneath the dotted line represents the deeper Connection between the leader and the ANC that drives the leader's willingness to overlook the ANC's behavior. This connection is the driving factor in these and many other kinds of workplace relationships. It seems that the deeper or the older the connection, the more outlandish the ANC's behavior can become.

Let's look at how this phenomenon tends to come to light.

How many times have you seen an unsuspecting company-man or company-woman challenge, correct, or discipline the inappropriate behavior of an ANC only to find that they (rather than the ANC) are receiving the rod of correction from the top? This scenario is a great example of why all my Culture Strategy Programs emphasize the importance of increasing your self-awareness and increasing your awareness of others. Whatever your role in the organization, be well advised when choosing to correct and address the behavior of certain ANCs until you are certain you know where they are receiving their orders and their support for the 'apparent' bad behavior.

Just make sure you look before you leap!

HINDSIGHT #30: STRATEGY BEFORE THE STRATEGY

Executing large scale and small projects can present a variety of challenges for any leader regardless of their personality type, strengths, or years of experience. Talented, goal-oriented, process-minded performers with great analytical skills must always remember how the human factor will impact their pursuit of operational success. How many times have you seen a leader or employee present a fabulous idea that contains a well-designed strategy and action plan, yet the idea is repeatedly delayed or totally dismissed?

The individual walks away from the experience scratching their head wondering what went wrong. Here's what probably went wrong in this scenario. The person with the great idea failed to do the strategy *before* the strategy. The person did not create a *People Strategy* before creating a *Process Strategy*. In organizations around the world, nothing is ever accomplished without relationships, and nothing challenges relationships like change does.

For those who are excellent at seeing how processes can be improved and productivity can be increased, they must remember that beyond things such as, capital equipment, physical resources, cash flow, and technology, relationships are the ultimate currency that drives all processes. Therefore, no process strategy is ever ready for design or execution until the right relationships are formed with the key people who can support it or shut it down.

Before you ever put pen to your 'process' paper, make adequate time to consider all the people who will and can impact the success of your plan. Be willing to take the time to build and leverage as many win-win-win relationships (a win for them, a win for your process, and a win for the organization) as necessary for the breadth, depth, and width of your process.

HINDSIGHT #31: LESSONS FROM A GREAT AMERICAN POET

Have you ever met a person who is blunt? This is a person who tells it like it is. This is a person who is not limited by the possibility that their honest opinion might crush your heart, your mother's heart, and the hearts of all those who care for you. Persons who are blunt can sometimes miss out on the upward mobility, personal grace, and limitless favor that many of their colleagues seem to enjoy, because the recipients of their unbridled realness are prone to things like reciprocation, revenge, and retribution.

I have found that there are many reasons why people are blunt. I was once a blunt person. One of my go-to lines was, "If you don't wanna know, don't ask." Can you imagine how many great opportunities I missed out on or how many hurt feelings I produced? It slowly became apparent to me that I was not using a popular and effective leadership mentality. I was not "winning friends and influencing people".

Brief Pause: If you have never read Dale Carnegie's book, *"How to Win Friends and Influence People"*, please check it out.

Instead, my bluntness was diminishing friendships and periodically enraging people. After a few run-ins with the negative results of my bluntness, I determined that I needed to adjust my communication style. But I could not adjust my communication style too far over to the land of 'fakeness' because I cannot stand fakeness or fake behavior. Can you? Fakeness produces sort of a 'pukey' (my word for vomit-inducing) feeling. I haven't met anyone who can stand fakeness. However, it's all around us.

I have spoken with countless leaders who struggle with playing the political game in such a way that they don't know how and where to land between being blunt, and seeming and feeling fake. I suggest that the midpoint between being blunt and being fake, which provides the best return on your investment of interaction with others, is *wisdom*. I think wisdom is knowing what God would want you to do in every situation: easy and manageable situations, complex and challenging situations, and scary and devastating situations. In many cases, wisdom is an appropriation of the insight we learned from the great American poet, Mr. Kenny Rogers, who said,

"You've got to know when to hold 'em
Know when to fold 'em
Know when to walk away
And know when to run
You never count your money
When you're sittin' at the table
There'll be time enough for countin'
When the dealin's done."

Wisdom is the instance-by-instance insight you need to make the best decision that advances your cause, connects you with the other person, and increases your knowledge and understanding. Wisdom is the instant ability to weigh and judge both the short-term and long-term benefits or disadvantages of your actions.

Wisdom helps you determine if you should stand your ground on your point of view, style, or approach or if you should acquiesce in some way. The most effective leaders have learned how to walk the fine line between brutal honesty and diplomacy which is a powerful blend of wisdom and finesse that enables you to be a straight-shooting -tell-it-like-it-is-realist who doesn't burn bridges in the process.

DY TRAFFIC LIGHT ACTION PLAN

Your willingness to be hungry, humble, honest, and helpful in your growth process will positively impact you and everyone you encounter. Take time to review your thoughts and notes to identify the insights that struck you.

Use the Traffic Light Action Plan to convert those insights into action steps you will Start Doing, Keep Doing, and Stop Doing. Use your calendar to plan when, how, and where you will take action!

START DOING	WHEN, HOW, WHERE
_____	_____
_____	_____
_____	_____
_____	_____
_____	_____

KEEP DOING	WHEN, HOW, WHERE
_____	_____
_____	_____
_____	_____
_____	_____
_____	_____

STOP DOING	WHEN, HOW, WHERE
_____	_____
_____	_____
_____	_____
_____	_____
_____	_____

Chapter 7: Help Your Team Grow

Hindsight #32: Reach Out. Reach Back.

Hindsight #33: Get to Know the Person Behind the Employee

Hindsight #34: Taco Motivation

Hindsight #35: A Reason to Make Your People Cry

Hindsight #36: They Will Be What YOU See!

Hindsight #37: No More Head Banging

Hindsight #38: If Jesus Had to Do It, So Must You

Hindsight #39: Using the Work to Develop the People

Hindsight #40: Specificity Is a Must

Hindsight #41: Make Delegation Developmental

Hindsight #42: Don't Fear Their Five-Year Plan

Scan the QR Code for My Personal Introduction to the Chapter!

Hindsight #32: Reach Out. Reach Back.

"Some of the architects and bishops behind a few of these great buildings are known, and much credit is given to them for their work, but the vast majority of the labor, the masonry, the carpentry, the stained glass was all done by people whose names history will never reveal."

Excerpt from *The Invisible Woman*, by Nicole Johnson

Here's a fun thing to do that feels good and often produces a powerful impact on others. Periodically thank, praise, and encourage the behind-the-scenes people who help you or have helped you. Receptionists. Administrative Assistants. Analysts. Why? It's right. It makes people feel appreciated. It plants good seeds in the ground for you. And don't you like it when people thank you for your efforts?

I'm reminded of an instance when I elected to contact the receptionist for one of my largest clients. Because I worked with people from several areas of the company, I often found myself speaking with the receptionist to make connections. She was always positive, always helpful, always polite. So one day, I called the company's main number and on cue, she answered,

Linda (not her real name): "Thank you for calling ABC (not the company). How may I help you?"

DY: "Hey Linda this is Derek Young; how are you?"

Linda: "Oh, hello Derek, I'm doing well; how are you today?"

DY: "I'm fantastic!"

Linda: "How can I help you Derek?"

DY: "Oh, I don't need anything. I just called to hear how you are doing and tell you how much I appreciate you."

Linda (Slightly startled): "What?"

DY: "Yes, I just wanted to let you know that as an independent business owner who deals with a variety of people from a variety of organizations, it is a real blessing to speak with someone like you. You're always so nice and so helpful. I just wanted to let you know that I really appreciate that, and I don't take it for granted."

Linda (Now crying): "Wow, no one has ever done that."

DY: "Well, that's not because you don't deserve it."

Linda: "Wow!" "What can I do for you?"

DY: "That's it. Have a blessed day."

Linda (Still crying): "OK, Thanks! Good-bye!"

Make time in your schedule to reach back and reach out to the people on the front lines and behind the scenes and thank them! You might be the first person who has ever done that for them.

Hindsight #33: Get to Know the Person Behind the Employee

I have a lot of love for our clients who lead teams because leadership is hard.

Side note: That should probably be its own book title and book focus, LEADERSHIP IS HARD!

Our clients are called to handle hundreds of issues, oversee hundreds of activities, manage hundreds of relationships. They are usually asked to accomplish these things with less time than they need and with fewer resources than they need. For example, we know that—generally speaking—each generation thinks and works with different standards; we know that unique groups and sub-groups in every organization want policies that address their unique needs; and we also know that what is right for one group may be ridiculous to another. Therefore, it is paramount that leaders understand what makes each person on their team tick.

These realities and others just like them are what lead me to encourage my clients that no matter what else is going on, they must make time to get to know the 'person behind the employee'. Their unwillingness to get to know their people will only complicate every other aspect of their work. Here are a few of the questions I ask my clients to help them clarify the importance of getting to know the 'person behind the employee':

1. How can you trust or be trusted by someone you don't know?

2. How can you motivate someone if you don't know what motivates them?

3. How can you effectively reward someone (the reward not only recognizes their accomplishment, but it incentivizes and inspires them to repeat or exceed the accomplishment) if you don't know how they like to be rewarded?

Ultimately, the process of getting to know the people on your team enables you to better leverage your work relationships.

Hindsight #34: Taco Motivation

After 40 years of working with and for a wide array of people from a wide variety of backgrounds, there are few experiences that have cemented some of my beliefs about people skills like this one. Several years ago, I was conducting a leadership presentation for a group of big-box retail store leaders. Among the participants was a tall, jovial, self-deprecating gentleman I will call Joel. Joel oversaw a strong performing department within his store.

During the session, I advised Joel and his peers to make sure they meet with each of their direct reports to learn how they wanted to be rewarded for exceeding their goals. I even walked through an exercise to demonstrate some of the ways they could conduct that interaction. Several weeks after the session, Joel said that he was surprised when he asked his high-end television section leader how he wanted to be recognized for beating his sales increase goal. His response was, "I want a taco bar."

Shocked by this response, Joel said, "A what?" The section leader replied, "A taco bar. I've always wanted a taco bar at work." Still caught off guard by the response, Joel repeated his inquiry,

"If you beat your sales increase goal in January, you want a taco bar as a reward?"

"Yes, that's right."

Joel told me that as far as he was concerned, he would give him taco pizza, taco sandwiches, and whatever else he wanted if that was all it took to produce that level of commitment. Equally shocked by the response, I marked my calendar to call Joel near the end of their fiscal year to check on 'taco man'. So, in December of that year, I called Joel to check on their progress. Excitedly and enthusiastically, Joel told me that the section leader not only beat his sales goal, he beat the goal in October.

I then asked Joel how the taco bar was received. Flippantly, Joel said he did not provide a taco bar. "What?" I asked, demonstrating my surprise and my disappointment that Joel didn't follow-through on his employee's simple request. Just before I could challenge Joel on his decision, he told me, "I didn't do the taco bar because his co-workers did it.

Some of his teammates heard about the taco bar challenge, and they did it for him. It was a big hit, and he was extremely excited about it." After Joel's report, I thought about the positive outcomes of this approach for Joel: one conversation, no new expense, teammates supporting each other, and sales increasing. This is life at its best for a leader.

This example often leads some to ask, "What if my employees want something I can't provide; something that's not feasible due to budget constraints, timing, or appropriateness?" Knowing how a person wants to be recognized positions you to do what they prefer and increase the likelihood they will deliver the performance you want. That said, wouldn't you rather know what they want so that you can set the parameters around what is possible for you to provide? Therefore, just keep talking with the employee until you can find rewards they want 'and' you can afford.

Let's look at it from a family point of view. If your child wants the new Blue Box 900 for Christmas at a cost of $1,000 but your holiday budget only allows $500 for a gift, you might ask if the Blue Box 450 will do. When leaders use this approach, they simply keep asking the person to share their preferred list of rewards until they identify a realistic and doable win-win option.

HINDSIGHT #35: A REASON TO MAKE YOUR PEOPLE CRY

The time spent with Joel and his fellow retail store leaders yielded another classic moment in my journey to help leaders achieve greater results. I shared another important recommendation with the group: Ask your employees what motivates them to do their best and include follow-up questions to uncover how they developed that motivation. Ask them! The subsequent conversation with one of the store leaders produced a real jewel that is described here.

DY: "Tell me your name."

Brian: "It's Brian."

DY: "How long have you worked for the company?"

Brian: "Twelve years."

DY: "You must have started right out of high school."

Brian: "Yes, I did."

DY: "Brian, let me ask you, what motivates you to do your best, to give your best effort?"

Brian: "I would say it's knowing that my boss is pleased with my work, knowing that Patrick (his district manager who hired me to work with his team) feels good about my work."

DY: "That's great Brian. Has anyone ever asked you that question?

Brian (with a puzzled look): "No."

DY: "Brian, how do you think you developed that motivation?"

Brian: "Well, it probably came from my time playing sports."

DY: "Ok, what sports did you play?"

Brian: "Oh, I played everything."

DY: "What would you say was your best sport?"

Brian: "Baseball!"

DY: "Were you a second baseman?"

Brian (Looking shocked): "Yeah, how'd you know that?"

DY: "I'm a big baseball fan, and you strike me (pun intended) as a middle infielder. So, I took a guess. Brian, what was it about baseball that led you to develop such a commitment to making your boss proud?"

Brian: "Well, my dad was my baseball coach for most of my little league career, and I always wanted to make him proud of me."

DY: "So your motivation for making your boss proud of you came from your connection with your dad through baseball?"

Brian: "Yessir!"

Note: Please notice that he did not say yes and sir as two separate words. Brian said 'yessir' as one word. If you're not familiar with southern communication patterns, I will tell you that when a man uses 'yessir' like that, it's all good in that conversation.

DY: "Wow! That's awesome. Let me ask you something Brian. What's your sales increase goal for this year?"

Brian: "We want to be up $2 million this year."

DY: "That sounds like a big goal. Just a second. Hey Patrick, let me ask you something. If Brian hits his $2M sales increase goal (this session was held one year after the great recession of 2007-2009) would you be willing to arrange a trip to your company's headquarters on the corporate jet?"

Patrick: "DY, if he adds $2M in sales in this economy, I'll give him a ride to headquarters on my back."

DY: "Ok. Wait. Brian, if you don't mind me asking, is your dad still living?"

Brian: "Yessir." (yeah, that's right it still applies)

DY: "So Patrick, if Brian hits his $2M sales increase would you be willing to write a letter to his dad saying how awesome his son is?"

Brian: (speechless, with tears in his eyes)

Patrick: "Certainly!"

A great lesson was learned.

If you have worked long enough, you know that some of the most popular motivators like more money, more responsibility, and more authority, do not work for every person. By asking about the origin of the other person's motivation, you gain deeper insight into the kinds of questions you should ask and the kinds of stories you should tell to help the person thrive. Save yourself some time and simply ask your people about their motivation! You might bring on a few tears in the process.

Hindsight #36: They Will Be What YOU See!

I have been blessed to have had the great fortune of working for legendary leaders like: Cal Turner Jr., the former Chairman, President, and CEO of Dollar General Corporation; Dr. Tom Hoenig, the former Vice Chairman of the FDIC and President of the Kansas City Federal Reserve Bank; and Don Turner, the former Chief Operating Officer for Cracker Barrel Old Country Store. As I consider my experience with and exposure to their leadership styles and many, many others, my understanding and expression of leadership has continued to grow and evolve. Among all the great leadership statements I have heard, one of my favorite leadership statements is the motto for 100 Black Men of America (The 100): "They Will Be What They See."

This statement emphasizes the idea that young people will emulate the attitudes and behaviors they see most often. As such, the members of The 100 strive to be positive role models for the young people they mentor. In the world of leadership, it seems that your team will not only become what *they* see but they will also become what *you* see. Just as leaders pursue a vision for their own lives, the vision they have for their team members helps to dictate how they treat those team members.

When a leader has a positive expectation for the outcomes associated with team members, that leader tends to look on the bright side and turn lemons into lemonade when negative events occur. Have you found this next point to be true? I have found that when a client demonstrates hunger *and* humility to learn and grow, my efforts to help that client are intensified. My process begins with establishing a positive vision for the person's future performance. I schedule meetings, create development plans, and conduct one-to-one coaching sessions with the belief that positive, productive change is coming. Then, by making time to get to know the 'person behind the employee', I increase the likelihood that I will find motivators and reference points that improve my connection with the client.

This process further increases opportunities for effective communication and partnership. While having an open mind about a client's potential does create greater opportunity for success, it is not an automatic pathway to success. Once the vision and goals for growth are set, the work of pursuing development is the next step. So, in your role as a leader of people, consider viewing yourself as their coach who sees their potential and interacts with them accordingly.

HINDSIGHT #37: NO MORE HEAD BANGING

Have you ever had an employee who makes you feel like banging your head against the wall? If you haven't had such an employee, be thankful for it and be prepared if you ever get one. One of the lessons I wish I had learned before I left college to start my business career is a simple one. It is not enough for the leader to have a clear view of how they perceive each team member's level of performance. It is much more important that the leader has a clear view of how the employee perceives his or her performance in relation to the leader's standards. How many times have you observed this scenario?

Example: Tabitha, the Senior Manager of Product Replenishment views herself as a 4 out of 5 or 5 out of 5 on every item in the Annual Performance Review Form. Tabitha believes she is a real gift to the department and a real treasure to work with. Unfortunately, Tabitha's boss, Keisha views her as a 2 out of 5 on most performance review items; and some of her teammates are amazed Tabitha still has a job.

This imbalanced view of Tabitha's performance rests on the shoulders of Keisha, the leader. Part of the leader's role is to ensure that each team member understands how they are performing from the leader's point of view.

In my Culture Strategy Program, entitled **Winning Teams Winning Ways**, we give leaders an easy to use process for rating and describing performance that helps them stay on the same page with their team members. One valuable part of that process involves the leader asking their employees this question, "What are some of the things you did to achieve your goals that I was not able to see?" Time after time, we find that this question generates many an 'aha moment' for leaders and often increases their respect for their employees. And at a bare minimum, this process either reduces or eliminates the head banging.

HINDSIGHT #38: IF JESUS HAD TO DO IT, SO MUST YOU

Michael Jordan (MJ) had to do it. Abraham Lincoln had to do it. Even Jesus Christ had to do it. Great leaders adapt to their teams. Great leaders understand that winning often requires that they diversify how they interact with their team to match the diverse talents, perspectives, and personalities of each member of the team.

Before adopting this attitude, MJ was a 63-point scoring, between the legs dribbling, crazy shot-making, playoff game-losing, superstar who could not win a championship. After converting his mindset to lead by adapting, he went on to win six championships.

Relying solely on his own talents and ideas, Abraham Lincoln was a multi-political race loser. After converting his mindset to lead by adapting, he won the largest political race in the world and engineered one of the most significant national transformations in history.

In a phenomenal sermon, Pastor James MacDonald of Harvest Bible Chapel in Chicago, demonstrated how Jesus used different tones, different words, and different methods to call each of the disciples to join Him in His journey to change the world. Jesus realized that each disciple had a different temperament, a different set of fears, and a different focus in life.

Your ability to adapt to your people will be much more fruitful than deciding to treat every person and every team the same way. I have seen the negative results that occur when a leader will not adapt to the uniqueness of each team member. When I compare the more successful leaders to those who tend to underperform, the message is clear: Winning often requires you to pass the ball and score 30 points rather than dominate the ball and score 63.

HINDSIGHT #39: USING THE WORK TO DEVELOP THE PEOPLE

Defining leadership is easy: influencing others to act (insert your definition here). Defining effective leadership (which can be directed by evil or good intentions) is not so easy. I believe the *process* of leading others and the *purpose* of leadership are different.

Years ago, I found a statement that summarizes what I see as the purpose of leadership: "Using the work to develop the people." Though I believe the major goal of leadership is about getting things done, I believe the ultimate benefit of leadership is the life-changing effect it has on the people you are leading and the people they are serving. When your team knows that you care about their well-being and their success, they are more willing to offer their best effort. When they know that you are not using them to get the work done but using the work to help them grow and improve, they become more excited about the tasks at hand.

The model in the picture below is a tool I use to help clients understand this perspective on leadership. The role of the leader is to help the team develop the knowledge, skills, confidence, network, and resources necessary to satisfy the customer. While the phrase "the customer is always right" has been quoted for many years, I much prefer the notion that if I take excellent care of my employees, customers will rarely feel the need to prove they are right. In the model below, the leader is at the 'bottom' of the triangle. Why? There are three major reasons:

1. The first reason is that the leader, especially in large organizations, often has no direct contact with customers and should therefore have a vantage point or method that enables her to see all the people on the team.

2. The second reason is that the leader is the only person who has full responsibility for all the outcomes of the operation, and thus has the widest span of control (represented by the horizontal arrow).

3. The third reason is that a leader's role is to serve rather than to be served. Placing the leader at the bottom of the triangle is a visual way to represent that.

DIAGRAM 2: YMG LEADERSHIP TRIANGLE®

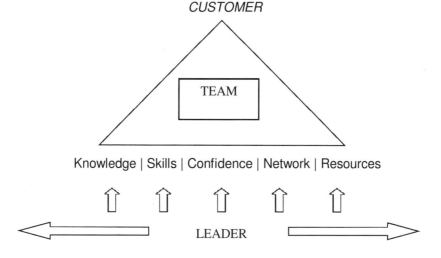

HINDSIGHT #40: SPECIFICITY IS A MUST

Good leaders praise their people when they deserve it. Great leaders praise their people before and when they deserve it. Legendary leaders provide 'specific praise' all the time. In addition to giving your team and your peers general praise (e.g. "Thanks for your hard work today!" "I really appreciate your commitment!" "Great effort out there!"), give them specific praise. Use descriptive and detailed language to describe what you're praising and why you're doing it.

Specific praise is a way to simultaneously recognize a person, teach your philosophy, and remind your team of the behaviors you want them to repeat. Specific praise informs your team that you are paying attention to them, and you care about their efforts. Compare the following examples and consider how each approach might impact your team members.

General praise: "Steve, I really appreciate your effort this week, and I hope you have a great weekend."

Specific praise: "Steve, not only did you help the customer become calm enough to really hear your explanation of the problem, you called her back to confirm that we met her expectations. That's the kind of follow-through that will keep her coming back to us rather than the competition. I really appreciate your commitment to carrying out our values and our processes. Have a great weekend and ask Marita (Steve's daughter) to score a goal for me during her soccer game."

HINDSIGHT #41: MAKE DELEGATION DEVELOPMENTAL

You are busy! You are so busy you're overwhelmed. Your boss just added two new projects to your plate. Yikes!

Have you considered delegation? You probably have. But have you considered developmental delegation? In my Culture Strategy Program, entitled **Developmental Delegation**, I encourage leaders to reframe the way they look at and handle delegation. Delegating work to your team members is like teaching someone to drive a car. The goal of both processes is to help the other person become knowledgeable, effective, and independent.

Delegation is not dumping. Delegation is not giving people what you dislike the most. Delegation is an art that can simultaneously create more free space for you and expand your team's knowledge, skills, confidence, and overall impact. In this program, we ask clients to list their five to ten top responsibilities, then envision how their team members can take on an increasingly greater percentage of each responsibility over the next three to twelve months.

Next, we have them create an action plan to teach each and oversee how each team member performs every phase of the related responsibility and schedule time to review their progress. Just like the process you would follow to allow someone to start driving in small chunks to giving them total access to drive your car, you control how much and how fast you delegate work to your team. That approach helps you maintain the comfort and confidence that your ultimate goals are being achieved...and no car wrecks are occurring!

HINDSIGHT #42: DON'T FEAR THEIR FIVE-YEAR PLAN

Do you have an employee who is new to you and your team or an employee you don't know very well? In the process of getting to know 'the person behind the employee,' I recommend using the following questions: "What is your vision for your career over the next three to five years? What do you want to do, and what do you want to become in 5 years?"

You might also add this phrase to your questions to gain greater insight about your employee, "...even if your career vision does not include this organization." I realize that question might scare or intimidate your employee. At some level, the employee might think, "Are you serious? I just got this job, and you want me to tell you that my long-term plan is to exit this place. Forget about it."

The person might not feel comfortable sharing their true answer for fear of retribution or dismissal of some sort. Employees who receive that question usually provide valuable personal insights that improve the leader's ability to show the link between the work goals and the employee's personal goals. Would you agree that your employees care more about their personal goals than your goals?

Exactly! I have seen the tremendous win-win impact of this approach. I'm reminded of a situation with an employee, we will call Omar, who joined the HR department of a large organization. Omar's manager asked him to share his 5-year vision during one of their initial status meetings. Omar paused briefly and then spoke openly about his goals. In sharing his five-year plan, Omar became most enthusiastic when he discussed his goal to become a manager of a human resource information systems (HRIS) function.

With that information in hand, Omar's manager found ways to assign him internal projects or include him in cross-functional projects that had an IT focus. In other instances, the manager involved him in meetings with the IT group so that he could learn how systems issues were handled.

Omar responded to his manager's commitment with a phenomenal work ethic, great team loyalty, and excellent productivity.

Five years later...

Omar's manager had moved on to a new organization when one day she received a phone call from a recruiter seeking a job reference for, *you guessed it,* Omar.

Note: Did you notice that the manager left the company before Omar had a chance to consider leaving. This is one of the many reasons I recommend you consider asking your employees about their longer-term goals to create greater understanding and commitment.

The job was, *you guessed it,* HRIS Manager. This occurred almost five years to the day Omar and his manager discussed his five-year plan. Omar got the job!

What a 'win-win-win'! Win number one: Omar received great experiences that prepared him for a personal goal. Win number two: the manager achieved her results partially due to Omar's commitment. Win number three: Omar was able to live out the statement, "success is where opportunity and preparedness meet."

DY TRAFFIC LIGHT ACTION PLAN

Your willingness to be hungry, humble, honest, and helpful in your growth process will positively impact you and everyone you encounter. Take time to review your thoughts and notes to identify the insights that struck you.

Use the Traffic Light Action Plan to convert those insights into action steps you will Start Doing, Keep Doing, and Stop Doing. Use your calendar to plan when, how, and where you will take action!

START DOING	WHEN, HOW, WHERE

KEEP DOING	WHEN, HOW, WHERE

STOP DOING	WHEN, HOW, WHERE

Chapter 8: Hold Your Team Accountable

Hindsight #43: There's A New Principal in Town

Hindsight #44: Have You Told Them?

Hindsight #45: Correct Quickly—Praise Quicker

Hindsight #46: Relevant, Relatable Analogies

Hindsight #47: Please, No More Surprises

Hindsight #48: Leaders Provide Constructive
Feedback

Scan the QR Code for My Personal Introduction to the Chapter!

HINDSIGHT #43: THERE'S A NEW PRINCIPAL IN TOWN

Have you ever been called to the principal's office? For those who have never had to take that long scary walk, it is a real stress-builder (I'll have to tell you about my trip to Mr. Brown's office some time). If you're a leader in an organization of any size, your office can sometimes feel like the principal's office. Why? In so many cases, leaders tend to use their office *only* for corrective and disciplinary actions. Even though that approach far outweighs correcting and disciplining people in front of their peers and customers, I hope you will start using your office as a place for specific praise much more than a place for correction and discipline. Over time this might make it easier for your team to receive correction when it is necessary.

HINDSIGHT #44: HAVE YOU TOLD THEM?

Here's the scene. It's Monday morning. Keva, the manager of the Finance team, is standing next to the coffee maker waiting for the cup to fill with java when Juan, the manager of the Accounts Payable team, joins her. Before Keva can pick up her cup, Juan starts commenting on all the things that Barbara, his vendor payables lead, has done wrong over the past two months. With great verve and detail, Juan provides a *Harvard Business Review*-level breakdown of all that's wrong with Barbara. There's only one problem. He has not shared any of this with Barbara.

Here's how leaders lose points: They don't lead. They complain about their people. They berate their people behind their back. They fill the air with all that's wrong with their people. Instead, they should be helping their people establish SMART (Specific, Measurable, Attainable, Time - bound and Realistic) development plans to eliminate and reverse negative attitudes and behaviors. The next time someone corners you at the coffee maker, water cooler, elevator, or treadmill with a barrage of criticisms about one of their people, simply ask, "Have you told them?"

Hindsight #45: Correct Quickly—Praise Quicker

Here's a quick multiple-choice test. What would you do if you were visiting your friend's home for a nice dinner, and you saw their two-year-old son approaching their hot stove with his hand directed at one of the burners?

A. Tell your friend that their son is quite cute

B. Imagine the sound he will make upon impact with the hot burner

C. Stop him

Here's another multiple-choice question. What would you do if one of your direct reports rolled their eyes, sighed loudly, and reacted defensively every time a representative of another department asked a challenging question during an important meeting?

A. Ignore the person's behavior

B. Laugh uproariously at every gesture

C. Redirect the person's comments during the meeting and counsel them to change their behavior immediately following the meeting

What percentage of leaders would do answer C in the first scenario? One hundred percent! What percentage of leaders would do answer C in the second scenario? Less than one hundred percent.

Here are my three requests if you are a leader of people:

1. If you need to deliver correction to one of your team members, do so immediately (doing everything possible to maintain their self-esteem and dignity) to help in-

crease the likelihood the employee will not repeat the negative behavior;

2. Avoid being a 'hinter'; a leader who speaks in general and non-descriptive terms in the hopes that the employee will catch the hint about their mistakes; and

3. Keep two-year-old's away from hot stovetops.

HINDSIGHT #46: RELEVANT, RELATABLE ANALOGIES

When you are trying to ramp up your team's commitment to a project or initiative, consider using analogies that relate to their hobbies, interests, and background. In my Culture Strategy Program, entitled **Winning Teams Winning Ways**, we encourage leaders to develop a spreadsheet which contains pertinent information about each person on their team. We have found that this simple tool can rapidly transform the quality of leader-employee relationships and help transform the performance of a team. The process of getting to know the 'person behind the employee' equips the leader with the information and perspectives that can be used to connect with the team.

Here's an example to consider:

Imagine a situation where you have a lead supervisor on your team who is angry because you promoted one of her peers to the Department Manager job she thought she should have received; and it's having a negative effect on total team productivity. Because you are a major fan of famous Shakespeare plays like *Othello*, you use an analogy from that play about the anger Iago felt after Othello promoted Cassio to the Lieutenant job to help your lead supervisor change her point of view.

Only one problem. Your lead supervisor does not know about or even care about Shakespeare, Othello, Iago or Cassio, and when she hears the names Iago, and Cassio, she thinks you're describing a feud between two fashion designers. Now imagine that same lead supervisor is a big fan of NASCAR; so much so that she has Dale Earnhardt Jr.'s name and car number tattooed on her arm.

To increase the likelihood that your lead supervisor will understand and follow your direction on how her attitude is affecting total team productivity, it might be more effective to use an analogy about a NASCAR driver who feels slighted because he didn't get the ride in his NASCAR team's number one car because the team owner selected another driver. More than likely, this analogy will accelerate (pun intended) the lead supervisor's understanding of the issue and increase her appreciation of your perspective. Remember to use analogies that match your team members' backgrounds, hobbies and interests.

Hindsight #47: Please, No More Surprises

Do you remember your first performance review? Or maybe even your last performance review? What is the purpose of a performance review? From where I sit, the performance review is a leadership development tool a leader uses to ensure they stay on the same page with each member of their team. The performance review allows the leader and the employee to have a record of clear performance goals and work standards that help the company track the employee's impact on the organization and thereby, help determine how the employee should be compensated. The leader's year-end goal is to ensure that the ratings of the team members are accurate, and the team members understand the ratings. Every performance review I have seen uses a five-point rating scale.

Unfortunately, countless employees are still being shocked and frustrated by their performance reviews. Why is this happening? In my experience, many leaders use the performance review process as a time to present the employee with a laundry list of problems, mistakes, and gaps that they never shared during the year.

So how do we avoid this? I suggest the following ideas for your performance reviews. Upon establishing the annual performance goals with the people who report to you, make sure you are certain they understand their job requirements and your expectations of them. *Let me say that again.* If you are not 100% certain that each of your team members fully understands your standards, your requirements for success, your view of the outcomes they should produce, and the way they should go about their work, stop now, put down this book (come back to it quickly) and schedule one-to-one meetings with each person to clarify this with them. In addition to ensuring they understand your standards, you must also ensure that you understand their expectations of you.

Once that foundation is set, meet with your team members one-to-one at least once per quarter to review their progress on their job goals. Hold an honest and detailed conversation about their performance, allowing them to share their perspectives on their work and their environment. Why? If your performance review uses a five-point rating scale, you should be concerned whenever one of your performance ratings and one of your employee's personal ratings differ by two points or more.

If this happens, please try not to perceive that as your employee not being able to face reality but instead, perceive that as an opportunity for you to revisit their performance and improve how you confirm that they fully understand your standards and expectations. Stress the importance of more frequent follow-up conversations throughout the year to ensure you both stay on the same page. At the end of the year, your goal is that they are prepared and enthused to find ways to improve their performance based on your feedback. If this process is done well, your and your employees' view of their performance ratings should be nearly identical by year's end. There really should be no surprises.

HINDSIGHT #48: LEADERS PROVIDE CONSTRUCTIVE FEEDBACK

Great leaders understand that helping their employees grow and improve requires that they give them honest information about how they behave, how they produce, and how they are perceived by others. Even though hearing this kind of information can sometimes be hurtful, unsettling, and confusing, it is necessary for people who want to improve their performance and their results.

To help ensure that employees understand the vital importance of hearing honest information, we tell our clients to avoid two commonly used terms: Constructive Criticism and Negative Feedback. Why? Both terms are oxymorons in an environment of personal and professional growth.

Let's face it, there is nothing constructive about criticism; that's why we silently cringe when we hear the term. Film critics are not paid to build up directors and actors. That's why they are called critics. They focus on criticizing, not improving.

What is the thought about using negative feedback to describe how you want to help your team member grow? Leaders share honest information with their employees because they care about them, and they want them to thrive. For people who are serious about getting better at their work, there's nothing negative about that. That is why we suggest leaders tell their teams they want to share 'Constructive Feedback'.

'Constructive Feedback' implies that the information might be challenging to receive, but it is totally intended to be helpful and developmental rather than critical or disruptive. In one of my favorite Culture Strategy Programs, entitled ***Making the Bad Apples Good and the Good Apples Better***, we share that far too many leaders have never been trained to deliver constructive feedback. The program helps participants complete the following steps:

1. Prepare 'for' a constructive feedback conversation

2. Prepare 'the' constructive feedback conversation

3. Practice the conversation before delivering it to their employee

Notice that we use the word conversation rather than confrontation (conflict). We do this because most people I know feel tense when they hear the word confrontation. More importantly, when you consider the types of issues leaders need to address with their employees, how often is a confrontation necessary? In most cases, employees are repeating negative or unproductive behavior that requires a clear, calm, direct two-way conversation. These are the kinds of semantics that matter for leaders who care about their people.

DY TRAFFIC LIGHT ACTION PLAN

Your willingness to be hungry, humble, honest, and helpful in your growth process will positively impact you and everyone you encounter. Take time to review your thoughts and notes to identify the insights that struck you.

Use the Traffic Light Action Plan to convert those insights into action steps you will Start Doing, Keep Doing, and Stop Doing. Use your calendar to plan when, how, and where you will take action!

START DOING	WHEN, HOW, WHERE

KEEP DOING	WHEN, HOW, WHERE

STOP DOING	WHEN, HOW, WHERE

CHAPTER 9: MAXIMIZE YOUR MEETINGS

Hindsight #49: Meetings Are for Decisions

Hindsight #50: People Like Your Meetings

Hindsight #51: Get to Know the Grinch

Scan the QR Code for My Personal Introduction to the Chapter!

HINDSIGHT #49: MEETINGS ARE FOR DECISIONS

Raise your hand if you love meetings? What, no takers? Well, you probably don't hate meetings either. What you probably hate is consistently reconvening about the same topic(s) without coming to a meaningful conclusion or plan of action. You haven't lived until you attend a meeting about another meeting.

In a 2012 article, Dean Newlund, reported that "In the United States alone, an estimated 11 million meetings take place during a typical work day" [Newlund, 2012]. Imagine how the total number of meetings would grow if we included meetings held in China, Germany, and India.

This simple suggestion about meetings has helped many of my clients produce better results in shorter time frames. Here is the paradigm shift that makes all the difference in reducing your meeting count: *the purpose of a meeting is to decide something, not to discuss something!* Stop. Let that sink in. It seems to me that many people would say that the purpose of meetings is to *discuss* something. I think that might be a partial cause of our over-abundance of meetings.

What if we saw offices, hallways, racquetball courts, corporate jets, and company parking lots as the places for most of our discussion time? What if we were intentional in using our discussion time to be prepared to make the decision in the meeting room? What if we used time outside the meeting room to increase our understanding of the other person's perspective and responsibilities? What if we traded in gossip time for investigative time to learn the core issues affecting our decision-making process? What if we challenged extraverts and introverts, quiet people and big talkers, arrogant people and shy people to use the time between meetings to discuss the issues and ideas of significance so that our meeting time could be decision-centered? Organizational communication can be an interesting thing. Have you ever felt that the process is reversed: *the decision is made outside the meeting room and then the discussions ensue during the meetings*? How about we reverse that, so you have more time for the work you are paid to do!

HINDSIGHT #50: PEOPLE LIKE YOUR MEETINGS

Have you ever received feedback that makes you react as if you were reverting to your younger self? During my time as head of Diversity and Inclusion and Community Outreach for Cracker Barrel, one of my co-workers from another department told me, "People like your meetings." My initial reaction was, "Fa-real?!" While I was initially appreciative of the compliment, I had to process it to ensure that my leg was not being pulled.

When I asked why, my co-worker said, "Your meetings start and stop on time, and sometimes they end ahead of schedule. Plus, we get stuff done, and everyone knows who's who and what's what." Bam! That did it for me. Reflecting on the compliment, I realized that my philosophy on meetings was working.

If you are frequently responsible for assembling and leading internal or cross-functional teams, this suggestion could be a winner for you. When scheduling a meeting, schedule a start time and an end time and include an agenda. A grouping of people without an agenda with a start and end time is not a meeting, but a conversation.

If you think the meeting will require an hour, schedule ninety minutes. If you think the meeting will take two hours, schedule two and a half hours. Here's the logic behind this approach. Everyone likes to leave a meeting early. So, with this approach you usually have a leave-early built in; and you have a buffer in case you misjudged the meeting length.

Here is the next benefit of this approach. As soon as the meeting is over, you can use the remaining time to clarify and report responsibilities to all the participants. I would suggest you set, as a goal, that every team member will have the meeting minutes before they return to their office.

Here's another benefit of this process. Far too many of us have meetings that are scheduled back-to-back. By booking the extra thirty minutes to summarize and disseminate what occurred in the meeting, you also prevent yourself from being rushed for the next meeting on your schedule.

Hindsight #51: Get to Know the Grinch

Remember when I recommended that you not read over a section of this book too fast?
Note: The following piece of advice is neither a typo nor a mistake.

When you are responsible for leading a major change initiative, please consider including at least one employee with the personality of *"The Grinch"* as a member of the change team, especially in the ideation phase. Seriously DY? Seriously!

Trust me on this one. If you manage the interaction with the team member who has "The Grinch" personality effectively, their input can be very helpful in bringing balance and clarity to your change initiative. You can usually rely on that team member to provide an honest perspective, even if other team members won't. I suggest you encourage that team member (and the entire change team) to share *all* the reasons the idea will not work, *all* the similar efforts that have not worked in the past and *all* the negative effects this initiative will create if it is carried out.

Either on the same day or a short time later, reassemble the change team to create action steps for preventing and responding to the very risks and fears they shared earlier. Our clients have been amazed how some of their most negative and most observant team members show up in the second session with a fresh, "we can handle this" mindset.

In my Culture Strategy Program, entitled ***Preparing Your Team to Master Change, Challenge, Chaos, and Crisis.*** I offer mindsets and methods for assembling the right change team and creating a shared vision that will make the change process much more palatable for everyone involved...especially your Grinch.

DY TRAFFIC LIGHT ACTION PLAN

 Your willingness to be hungry, humble, honest, and helpful in your growth process will positively impact you and everyone you encounter. Take time to review your thoughts and notes to identify the insights that struck you.

Use the Traffic Light Action Plan to convert those insights into action steps you will Start Doing, Keep Doing, and Stop Doing. Use your calendar to plan when, how, and where you will take action!

START DOING	WHEN, HOW, WHERE

KEEP DOING	WHEN, HOW, WHERE

STOP DOING	WHEN, HOW, WHERE

CHAPTER 10: BONUS

Hindsight #52: 'Mother' Knows Best

Scan the QR Code for My Personal Introduction to the Chapter!

HINDSIGHT #52: 'MOTHER' KNOWS BEST

Among all the television shows that were made in the 1950s and rebroadcast in the '60s and '70s, few made more of a cultural impact on America than *Father Knows Best*. The show centered on the mundane and outlandish life experiences of what was largely portrayed as the 'traditional' American family. Though the show and its actors received great acclaim and I really enjoyed watching the show, the story lines contained in each episode never really matched my domestic reality.

Unlike the traditional family portrayed in the show, my immediate family was much different. My nuclear group included me, my mother and her mother—my Granny. When I examine how they raised me and how they advised me during my childhood, teen years, young adult years, and adult years, I am pleased to say that my mother and grandmother never gave me any bad advice. All their instruction, counsel, and correction has been positive and beneficial. Here are the top nine nuggets they shared with me that might help you in your career.

1. *"Be as nice to the janitor as you are to the president."*
2. *"You have to do what you have to do versus what you want to do!"*
3. *"Live by the Serenity Prayer!"*
4. *"When people say they're just playing, they are not playing."*

5. *"People may not like you, but they need to respect you."*
6. *"Whatever you do, don't become a complainer. It doesn't work and it will make people dislike you."*
7. *"Whatever you do, you have to learn how to deal with people."*
8. *"Find what you're good at and be the best at it."*
9. *"Watch as well as pray."*

Bringing it Home

I want to congratulate you on your commitment to your personal growth! I pray that the information in Make My Hindsight Your 20/20 increases your work success with your up line leaders, peers, teammates, partners, and customers. I also hope it helps you create and sustain new levels of joy.

To further solidify what you gained from this book, check out all my Culture Strategy Programs, professional webinars, and student webinars, at:

www.derekyoungspeaks.com

Every program and webinar is filled with hindsights similar to the ones offered in this book.

Finally, please share this book with others; especially those who are about to start their career journey. This book is a perfect gift for recent or soon to be college graduates, first time leaders/supervisors, and any person in need of career support or inspiration.

Be Legendary!
DY

BIBLIOGRAPHY

Bird, L., Johnson, E., & Macmullan, J. (2009) *When the game was ours:* New York, NY: Houghton Mifflin Harcourt.

Boone, D. (2014) *The way we work: How faith makes a difference on the job:* Kansas City, MO: Beacon Hill Press.

Calloway, J. (2009) *Becoming a category of one: How companies transcend commodity comparison:* Hoboken, NJ: John Wiley & Sons.

Carnegie, D. (1936) *How to win friends and influence people:* New York, NY. Simon & Schuster.

Fisher, B. & Fisher J. (2008) *Life is a gift: Inspiration from the soon departed:* New York, NY: Hatchette.

Giovani, N. (1997) *Love Poems:* Nashville, TN: HarperCollins.

Goldsmith, M. & Reiter, M. (2007) *What got you here wont get you there: How successful people become even more successful:* New York, NY: Hyperion.

Goleman, D. (2012) *Emotional Intelligence: Why it can matter more than IQ:* New York, NY. Random House.

Holy Bible, King James Version.

Irwin, T. Ph.D. (2014) *Impact: Great leadership changes everything:* Dallas, TX: BenBella.

Johnson, N. (2005) *The Invisible Woman: When only God sees:* Nashville, TN: Thomas Nelson.

Shakespeare, William, 1564-1616. (1975). Othello: 1622. Oxford: Clarendon Press.

Wilkinson, B. (2002) *Prayer of Jabez: Breaking Through to a Blessed Life:* Sister, OR: Multnomah.

Articles:

Newlund, D. (2012). *Make Your Meetings Worth Everone's Time.* Retrieved from https://usatoday30.usatoday.com/USCP/PNI/Business/2012-06-20-PNI0620biz-career-getting-aheadPNIBrd_ST_U.htm.

Movies and Television:

Capice, P., Katzman, C., Rich, L., (Producer), Katzman, L. (Director). (1978-1990). *Dallas* [Television series]. Dallas, TX: CBS.

Kennedy, K., Marshall, F., Mendel, B. (Producer), Shyamalan, M.K. (Director). (1999). *The Sixth Sense* [Motion Picture]. United States: Hollywood Pictures.

Naar, J.T. (Producer). (1975). *Starsky & Hutch* [Television series]. Hollywood: American Broadcasting Company.

Reiner, R. (Producer), & Reiner, R. (Director). (1992). *A Few Good Men* [Motion Picture]. United States: Columbia Pictures.

Music:

Can't Buy Me Love [Recorded by The Beatles]. On *A Hard Day's Night* [7-inch record]. United Kingdom: Parlophone.

The Gambler [Recorded by Kenny Rogers (Kenny Rogers)]. On *The Gambler* [audiophile edition vinyl]. New York, NY: United Artists.

Index

ACKNOWLEDGMENTS

First and foremost, I want to thank You, Lord God, for Your grace, mercy, gifts, and covering! Thank You for helping me help others!

Thanks to my wife Allyson and our children, Kayla, Kelton, Kendall, and Kristianna, for your constant love, support, and inspiration.

Thanks to my mother Jennie Young, my uncle Clinton Young, my Aunt Rosemary Walker, my cousin Carl Green, my Godmother and God-sister Shirley and Jennifer Whittaker, my sister Jeanie Campbell, and the entire St. Louis family for your constant prayer, encouragement, and support.

Thanks to Timothy O. Bond and Adrian Davis at True Vine Publishing for challenging me to expand the number of people I can help by sharing the 'hindsights' in this book.

Thanks to Chris Bond, Motelawah Smith, Jasmine Beard, and Kenny McEastland for making the visuals of this book support the essence of the message.

Thanks to my pastors, Bishop Horace and Elder Kiwanis Hockett, and Assistant Pastors Elder Harold and Marion Hockett for your prayers, support, and guidance.

Thanks to the greatest little sister ever, Anna Walker and my friends Janeth Brown, Alesia Johnson, and Angela Jones for more than a decade of encouragement to share life-changing information in written form.

Thanks to Bucky Rosenbaum for sharing your expertise in the delivery of this book.

Thanks to Suzi Earhart, Carolyn Foster, Adrian Granderson, Marcella Gravalese, Amy Henderson, Brian Hockett, Chip Hockett, Shay Howard, Alisha Keig, Andre Lee, Matt Moses, Mark Nave, Bobbie Porter, Diana Puglio, and Justin Robertson for investing your time and talent in this process.

Thanks to Dr. Bob Fisher and my friends at Belmont University for agreeing to host the book launch and partnering with me to help young people maximize their gifts through education.

Thanks to every person, known or unknown and near or far, who has prayed for my family and the impact of this book.

Finally, thanks to you for purchasing this book, sharing it with your family, friends, and colleagues, and joining the Hindsight Movement!

Be Legendary!
DY

VISIT
WWW.DEREKYOUNGSPEAKS.COM

FOR EACH OF THE FOLLOWING AND MORE:

MOTIVATIONAL KEYNOTES

CORPORATE CULTURE CONSULTING

DY'S STAY SHARP WEBINARS

MAKE MY HINDSIGHT YOUR 20/20
BOOK PURCHASE, SIGNINGS, AND KEYNOTES

CAREER DAY
with DEREK YOUNG
INFORMATION & INSPIRATION FOR YOUR SUCCESS

ASK DWHY
Real. Career. Solutions.

FIND ME ON

DEREK YOUNG
BE LEGENDARY!
www.derekyoungspeaks.com